IF ONLY MY MOTHER HAD TOLD ME...

(OR, MAYBE I JUST WASN'T LISTENING)

101

PEARLS OF WISDOM
I ENDED UP DISCOVERING
FOR MYSELF

BY DR. ROSIE KUHN

First published in the United States by The Paradigm Shifts Publishing Co.
PO Box 1637, Eastsound WA 98245
Cover design, formatting and editing by Maureen O'Neill,
www.onfirecoaching.com
(Fonts: Adobe Trajan, Trajan Pro and Microsoft Calibri)

ISBN: 978-0-9835522-2-2

ACKNOWLEDGMENTS

This book, *You Know You Are Transforming When...*, furiously flowed onto the pages. It is an incredible experience to essentially be just the conduit for the Universe's desire to create and to inspire. I'm so grateful to be useful to the Universe in this way.

Maureen O'Neill has been of incredible value in making this series of books beautiful and readable. She brings her heart and soul to the graphics of the cover design, as well as the formatting of each page, so that each phrase is a poem in itself. I'm so very grateful, Maureen for your loving support.

I also want to acknowledge, Jessica Ruby Hernandez, who always makes herself available for editing and consulting. I so appreciate Ruby's keen eye for detail and for her youthful perspective, which often reminds me that different generations have a different view of the world.

Without my relationship with my mother and with my two delightful children I wouldn't have experiences from which I've learned and have shared thus far. The role of parent and of child is rarely effortless, yet the gifts are incredibly rewarding. I'm grateful for the patience my parents and my children cultivated during our years together. I'm grateful for your willingness to endure what was not understandable, loving me through it all. Thank you.

DEDICATION

To Parents and Children.
We are all doing our very best.

INTRODUCTION

None of us ever decide to have children with the intention of screwing them up, or making their lives miserable or ruining any chance of their happiness. We never wish the worst on our children, like some black curse spat out into a cauldron. It just isn't like that.

The fact is, that the majority of us are created in the name of love. Our intentions for our little bundles of joy are largely the hope of a better life– better than what any of us survived.

The problem is, that the best that each parent brings to their role rarely meets the demands of their children. Life is so big. The complexity of even one human life is a lot to be with. How do any of us know what our children need or want from us?

I'm not sure what I needed from my parents, aside from food, shelter, some form of security and to hear "I'm proud of you." And I don't remember ever hearing from my parents how I might have made a positive contribution to their lives in some way, that I was a blessing in their lives. As the sixth of nine children, I often felt invisible and insignificant. My hope for my own life was that I would grow up, get married and have children of my own and that my children would know every day, all the ways they were special to me, all the ways they made a difference in my life. I would listen intently to hear what they needed and I would then lovingly fulfill their wishes.

As it happens, life turned out very differently from what I imagined. I don't know a parent that hasn't said at some point in their evolution through parenting, "I just didn't think it was going to be like this!"

We do the best we can. In hindsight, if we are wise, we see the impeccability of our parents' parenting in bringing us to the quality of wisdom and character that we bring to the world and to our children. We continue to pass on the best and the worst that our parents passed to us, until one day, we experience a level of awakening that stops us in our tracks. It is in this moment that we realize that we have capacities to choose that our parents and their parents never had. We have a higher degree of consciousness, knowledge, education and experience, which empowers us to love and care for our children in a better way. This is a good thing.

May this little book remind you of the many pearls of wisdom you have heard along the way, from parents, grandparents, teachers, siblings or simply discovered for yourself. And, perhaps there will be some here that you will happily pass on to your children, if they are listening.

***My intention for this book was not to be a journal, per se, yet it has, in its unique way, provided a space where journaling can take place. Enjoy the space in all ways possible.

IF ONLY MY MOTHER
HAD TOLD ME...

IF ONLY MY MOTHER
HAD TOLD ME...

DEEP, RICH & RAW
PRESENCE WITH LIFE
IS REALLY THE BEST
WE CAN HOPE TO EXPERIENCE.

#1

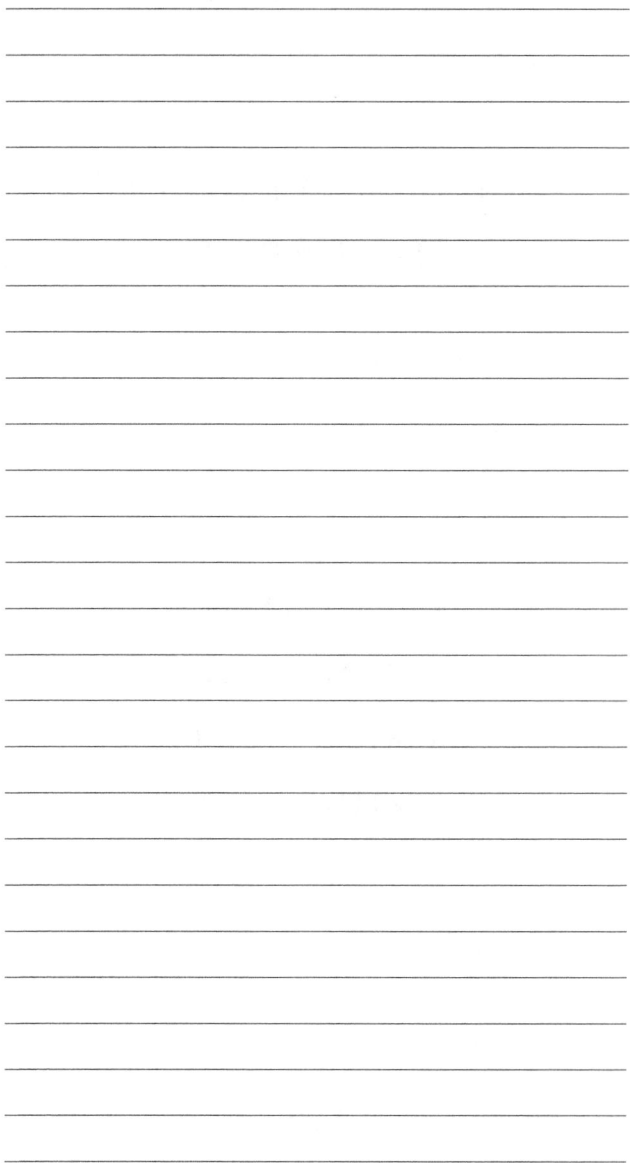

IF ONLY MY MOTHER
HAD TOLD ME...

LIVING LIFE
AS AN ADVENTURE
MAKES US YUMMY
& FULFILLED.

#2

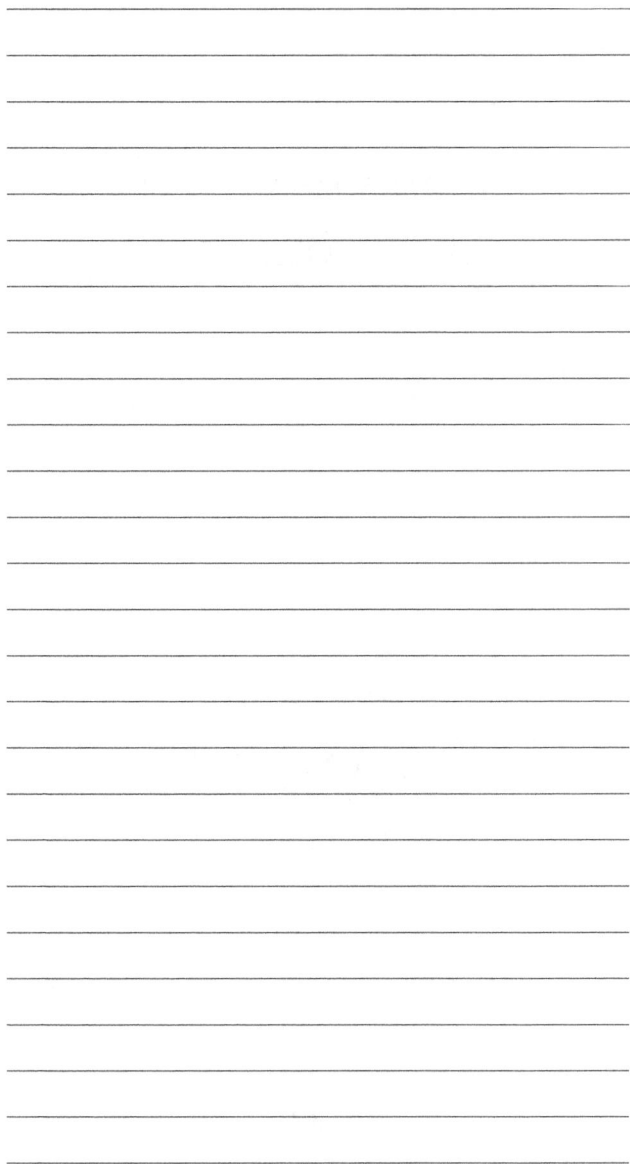

IF ONLY MY MOTHER
HAD TOLD ME...

ALWAYS
GO FOR THE
EXTRAORDINARY.

#3

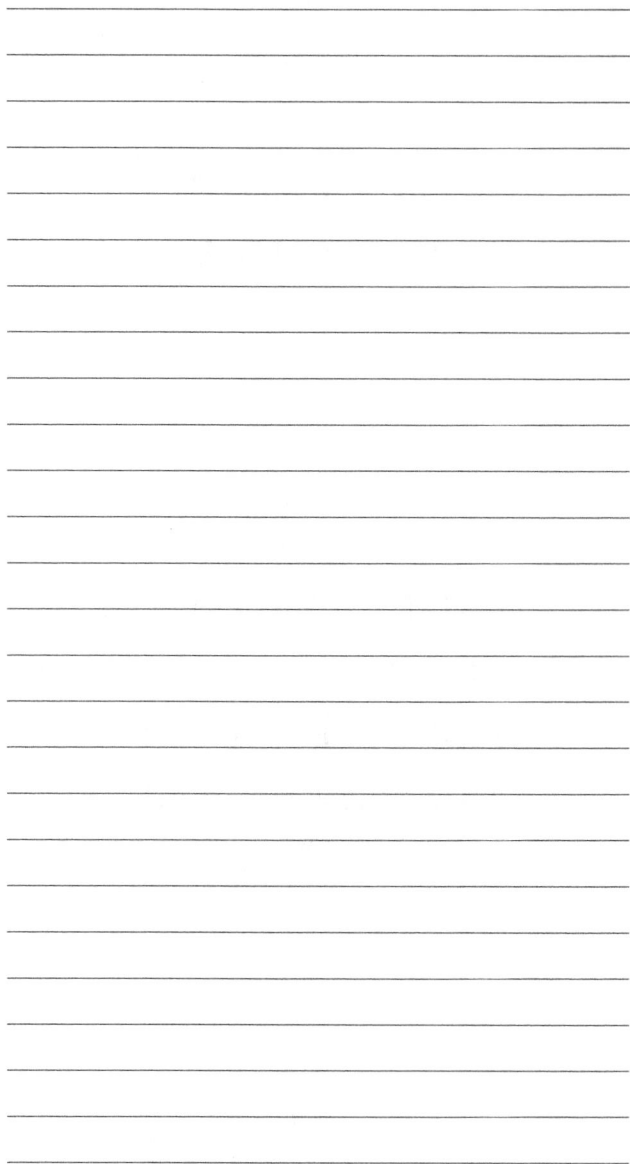

IF ONLY MY MOTHER
HAD TOLD ME...

TRUST YOUR SELF FIRST.
IF YOU DON'T TRUST YOUR SELF,
YOU WON'T BE ABLE TO TRUST
THAT YOU CAN TRUST OTHERS.

#4

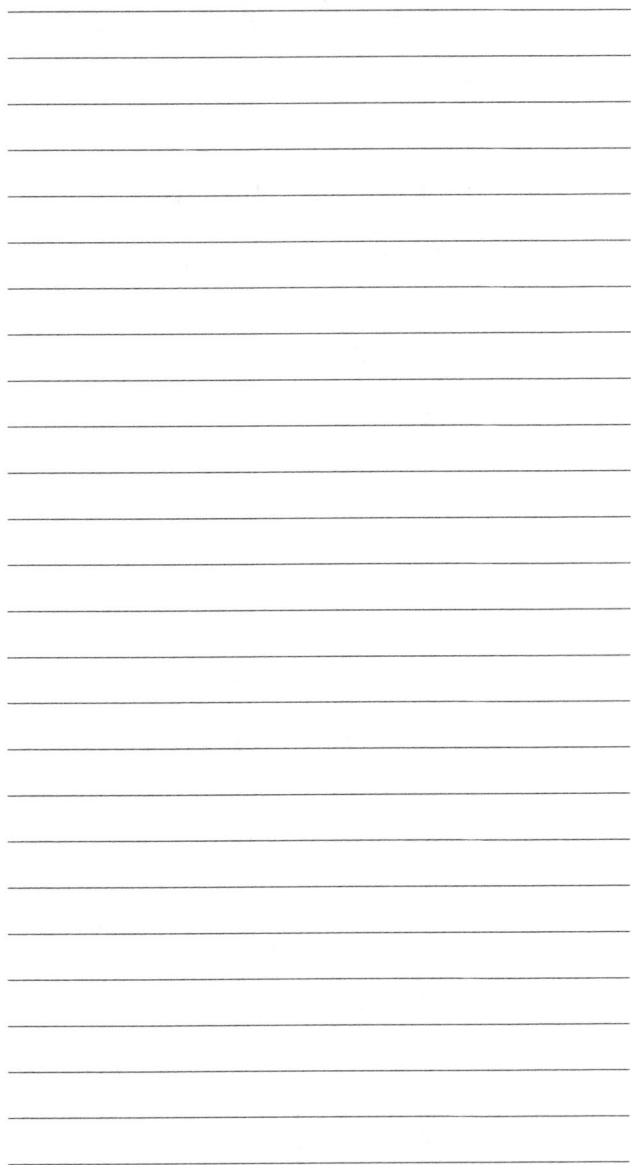

IF ONLY MY MOTHER
HAD TOLD ME...

YOU LACK
ABSOLUTELY NOTHING.

#5

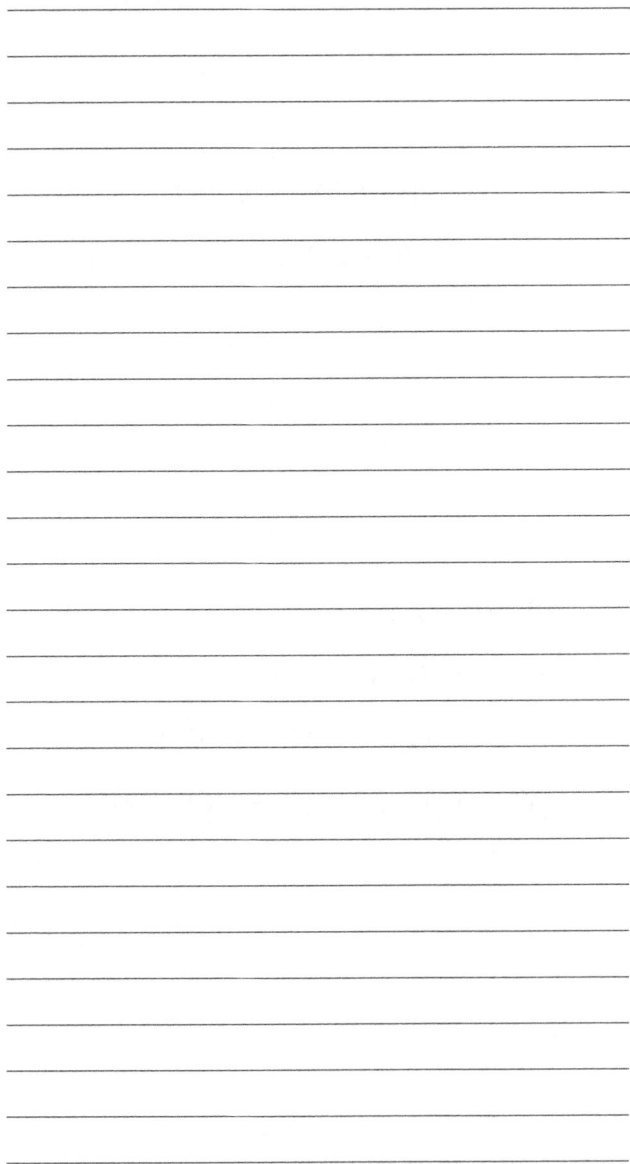

IF ONLY MY MOTHER
HAD TOLD ME...

DO WHAT I TELL YOU TO DO
ONLY WHEN IT IS
IN ALIGNMENT WITH
YOUR HIGHEST KNOWING.

#6

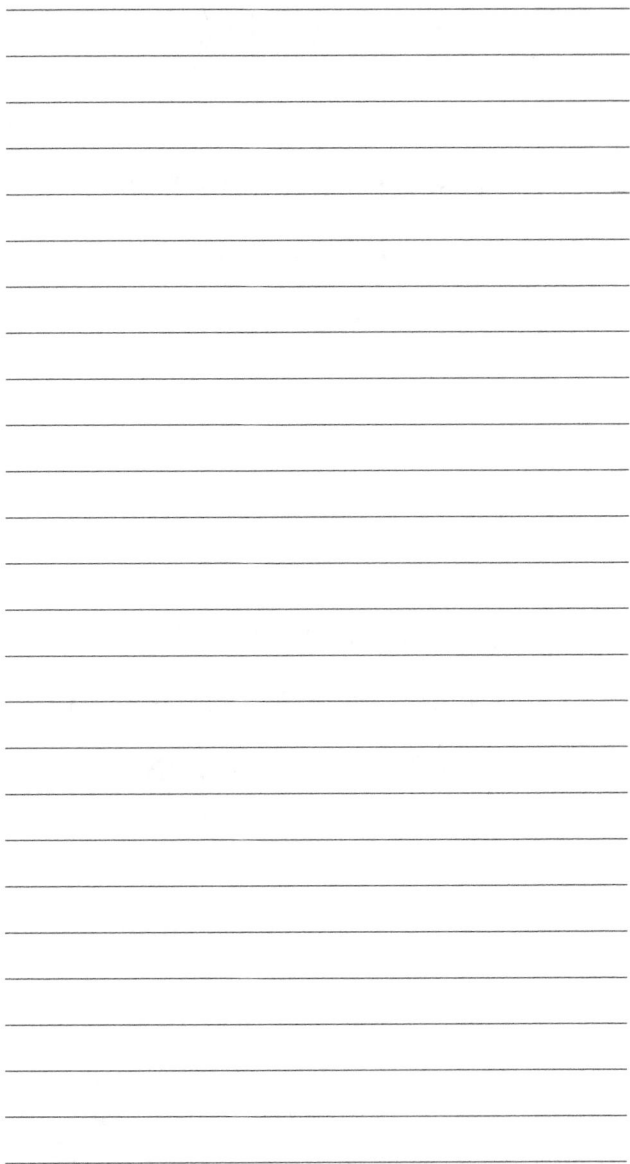

IF ONLY MY MOTHER
HAD TOLD ME...

LISTEN TO YOUR
INTUITION FIRST & ACT ONLY
FROM INSPIRATION.

#7

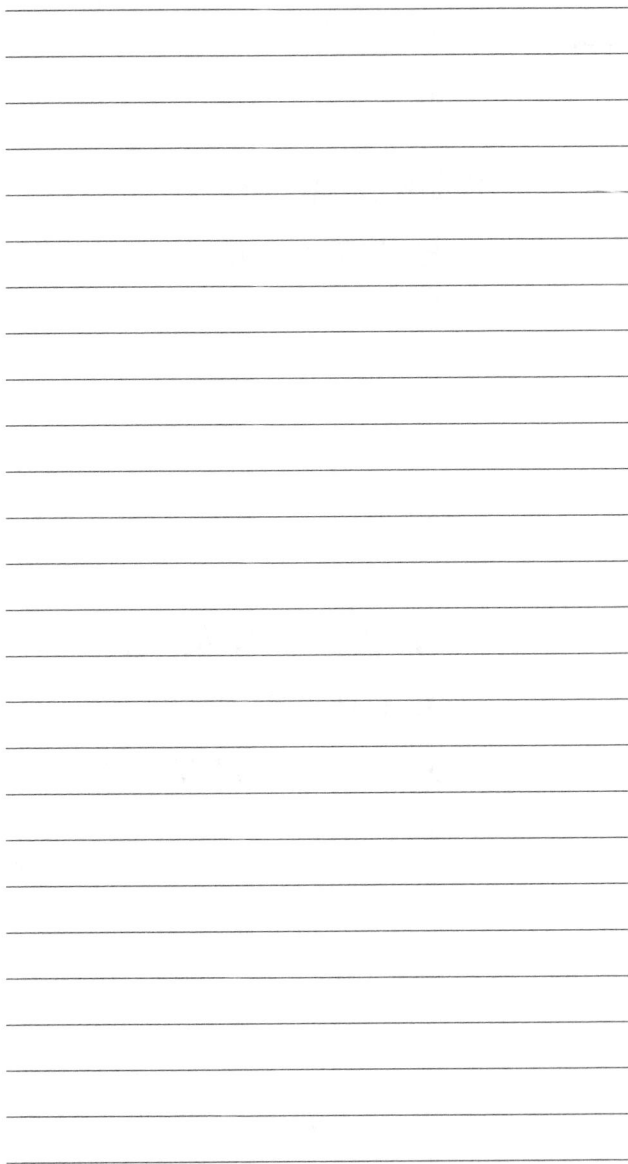

IF ONLY MY MOTHER
HAD TOLD ME...

RELIGION IS JUST THE BEGINNING
OF THE JOURNEY
INTO SELF-REALIZATION.

#8

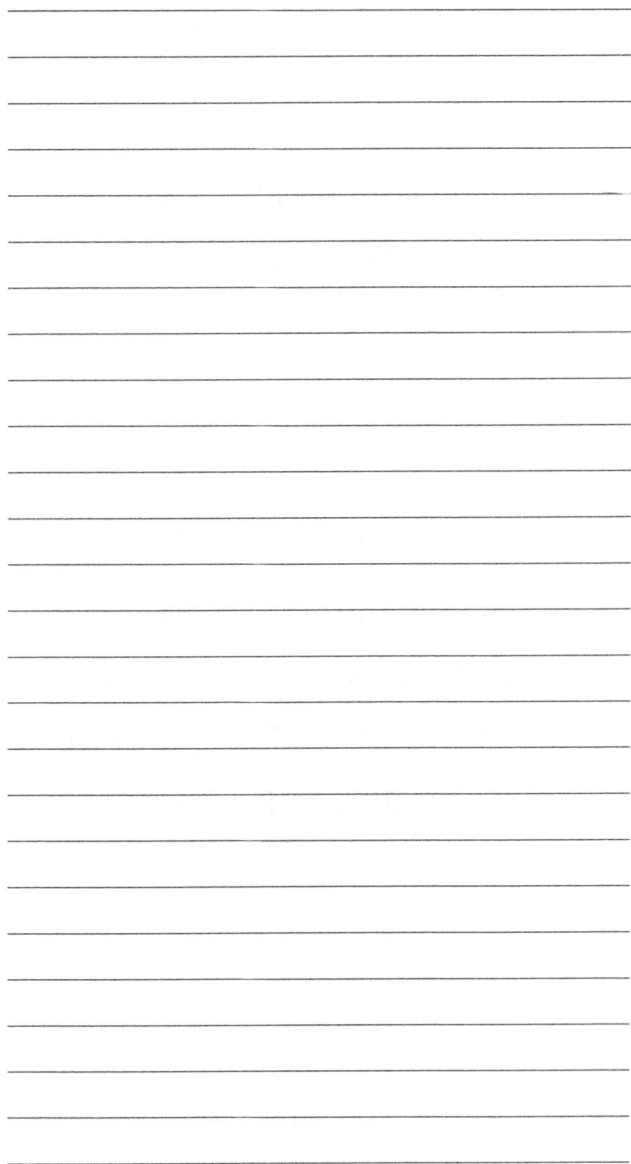

IF ONLY MY MOTHER
HAD TOLD ME...

DON'T BUILD YOUR LIFE
AROUND ONE RELIGION.
EXPLORE WHAT'S TRUE FOR YOU &
CREATE ONE FOR YOURSELF.

#9

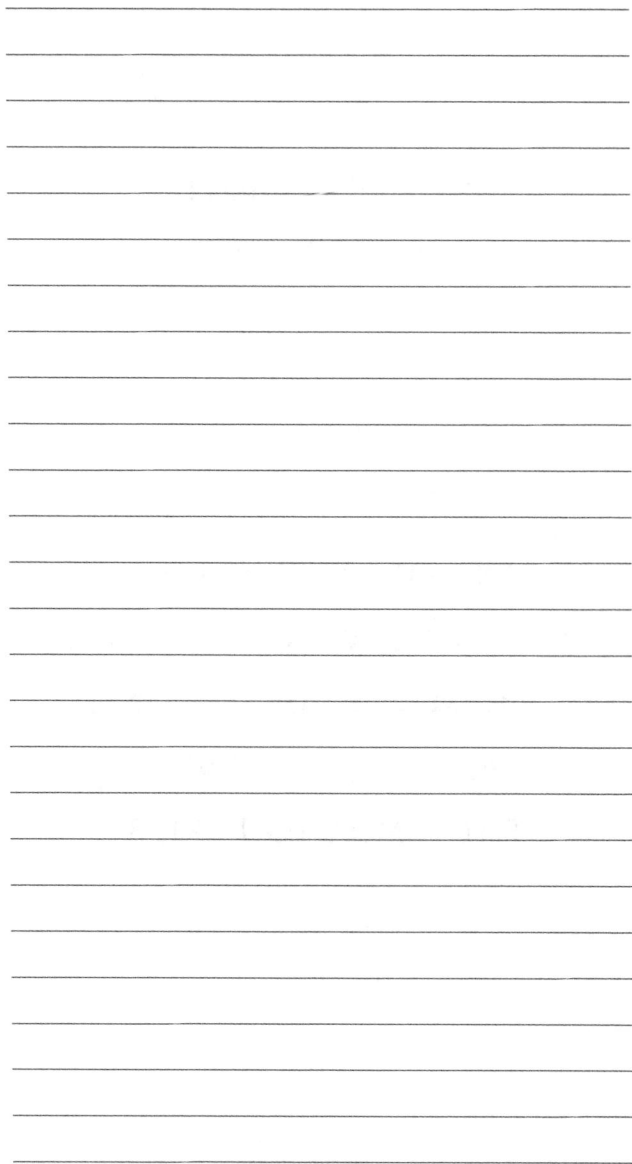

IF ONLY MY MOTHER
HAD TOLD ME...

EXPLORE THOROUGHLY
YOUR OWN WANTS & DESIRES,
YOUR OWN TASTES & STYLE,
YOUR OWN FRIENDS &
THE FAMILY YOU CREATE.

#10

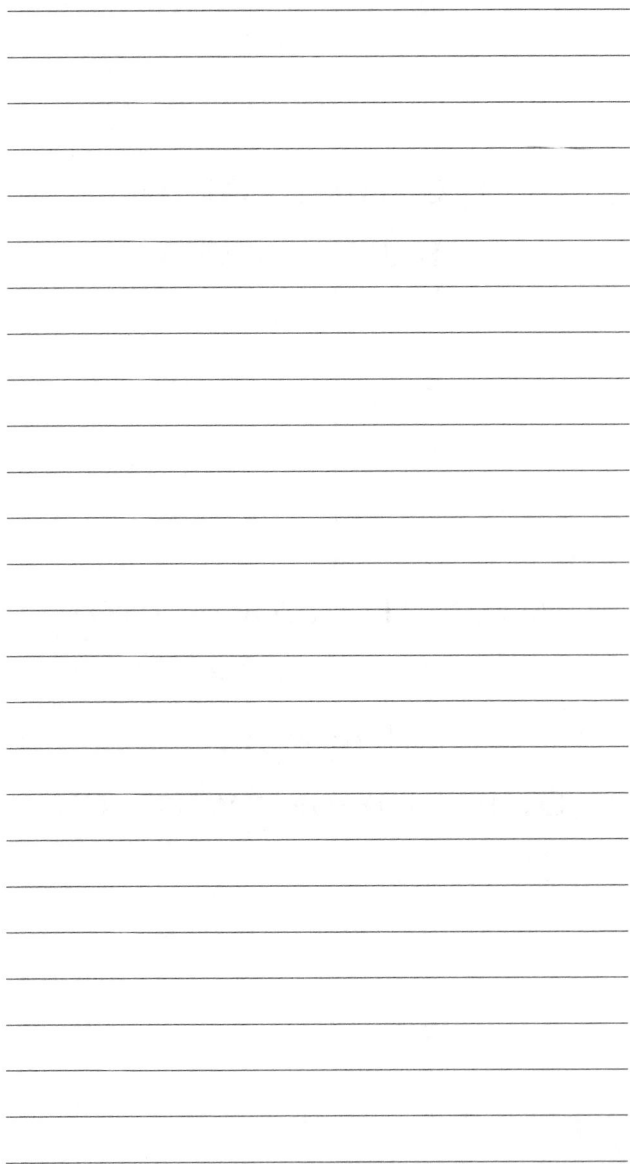

IF ONLY MY MOTHER
HAD TOLD ME...

ALWAYS SPEAK YOUR TRUTH,
NO MATTER
HOW MUCH
OTHERS DISAGREE WITH YOU.

#11

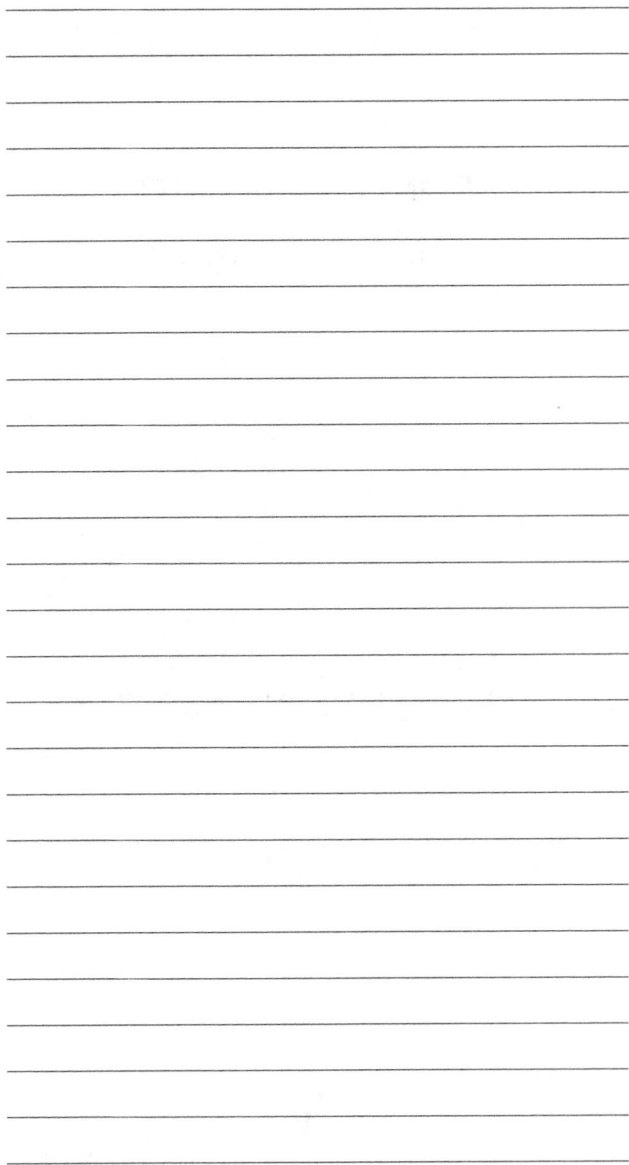

IF ONLY MY MOTHER
HAD TOLD ME...

DARE TO LIVE DIFFERENTLY.

#12

IF ONLY MY MOTHER
HAD TOLD ME...

NEVER LET YOURSELF
BE GUILTED
INTO DOING ANYTHING
YOU DON'T WANT TO DO.

#13

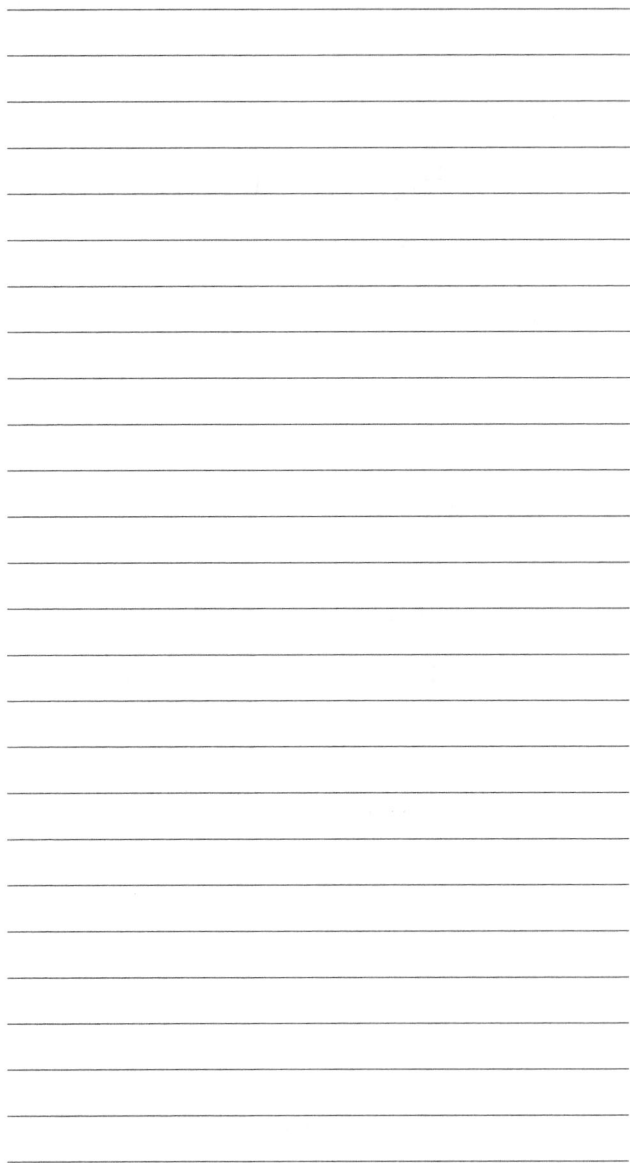

IF ONLY MY MOTHER
HAD TOLD ME...

FULFILL ONLY
THOSE OBLIGATIONS
THAT FULFILL
YOUR HEART'S DESIRE.

#14

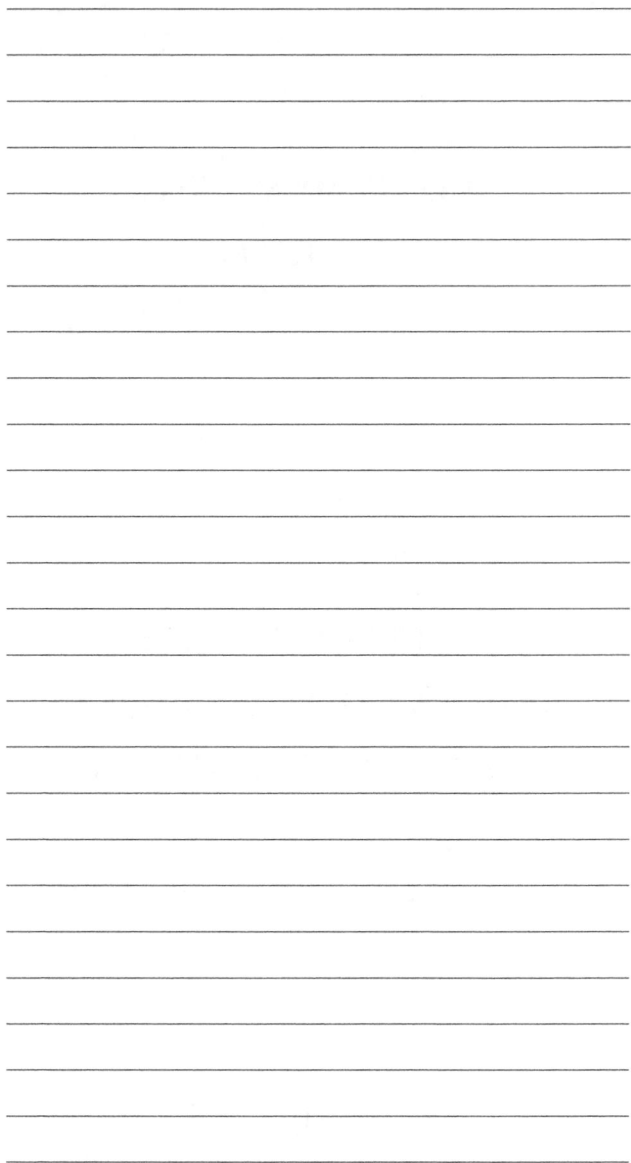

IF ONLY MY MOTHER
HAD TOLD ME...

THERE ISN'T REALLY
A RIGHT WAY TO LIVE, BE, OR DO.
THERE IS ONLY YOUR WAY.

#15

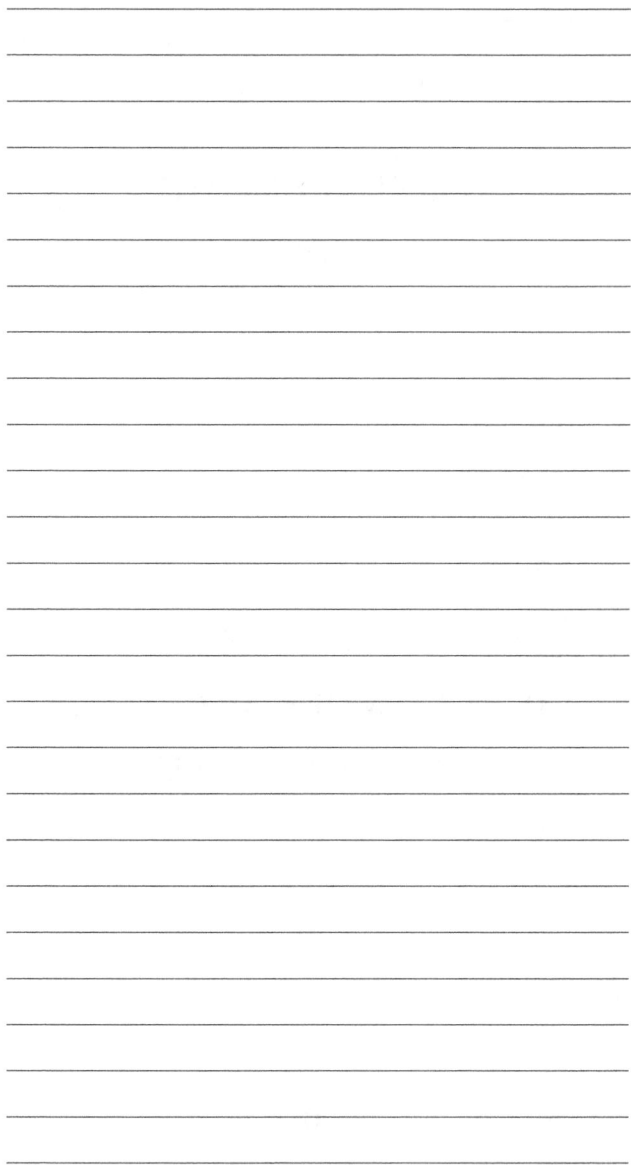

IF ONLY MY MOTHER
HAD TOLD ME...

LEARNING TO LOVE WELL
IS MUCH MORE IMPORTANT
THAN BEING LOVED.

#16

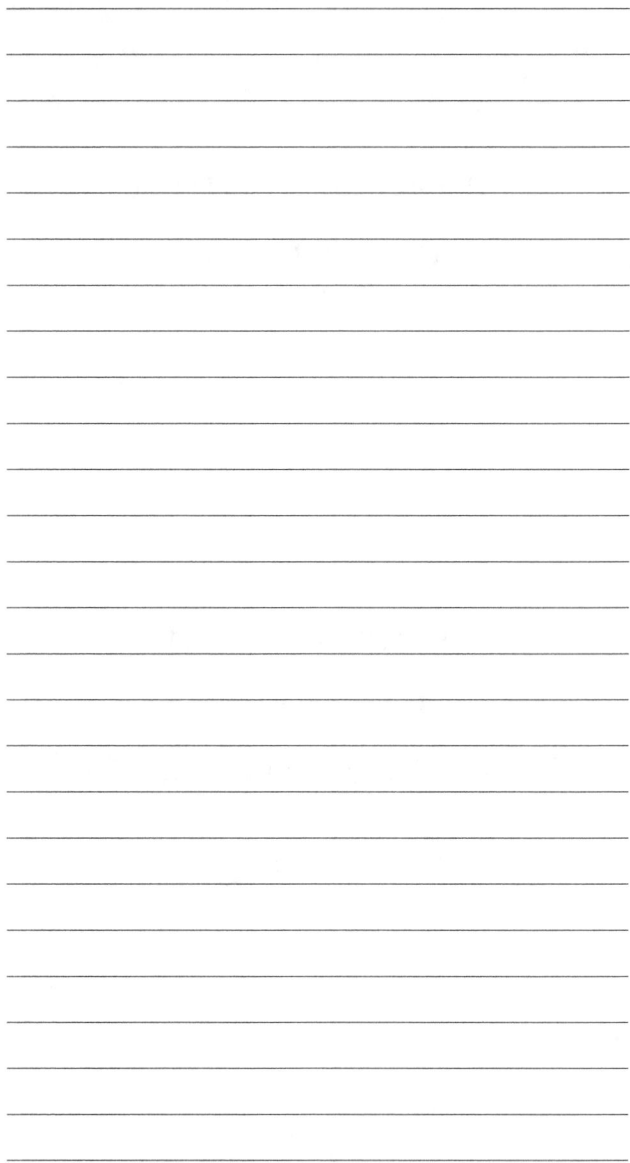

IF ONLY MY MOTHER
HAD TOLD ME...

I DON'T WANT YOU
TO BE LIKE ME.
I WANT YOU TO BE LIKE YOU!

#17

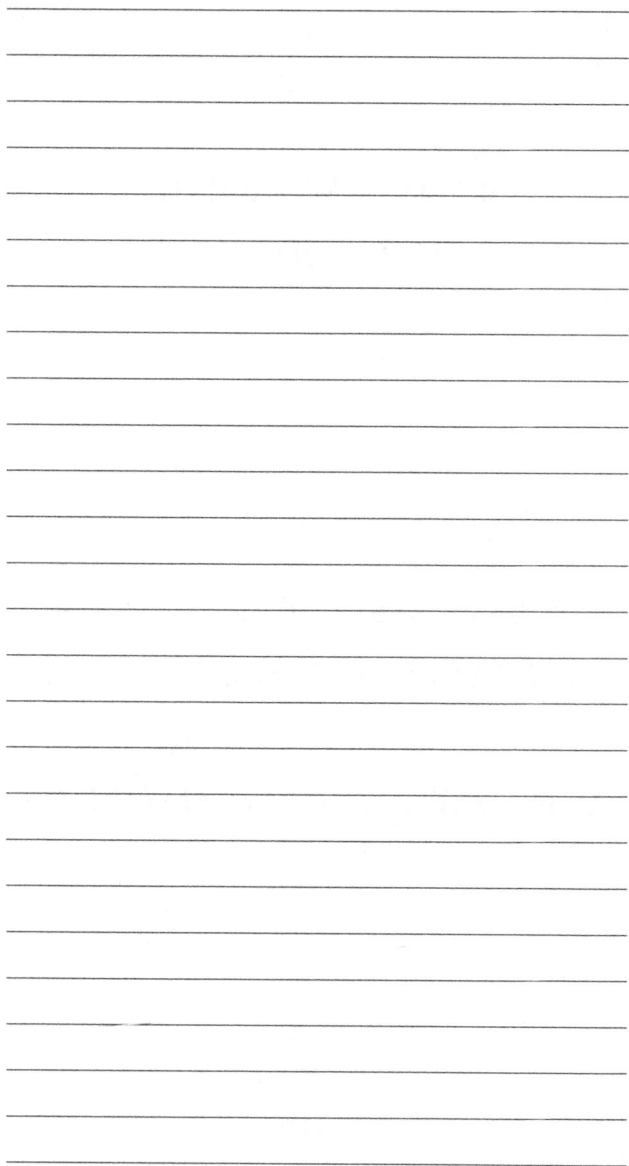

IF ONLY MY MOTHER
HAD TOLD ME...

LIFE IS MESSY, SCARY & HARD.
SOMETIMES YOU ARE GOING TO
JUST WANT TO DIE!
AND DEATH IS ALWAYS AN OPTION.

#18

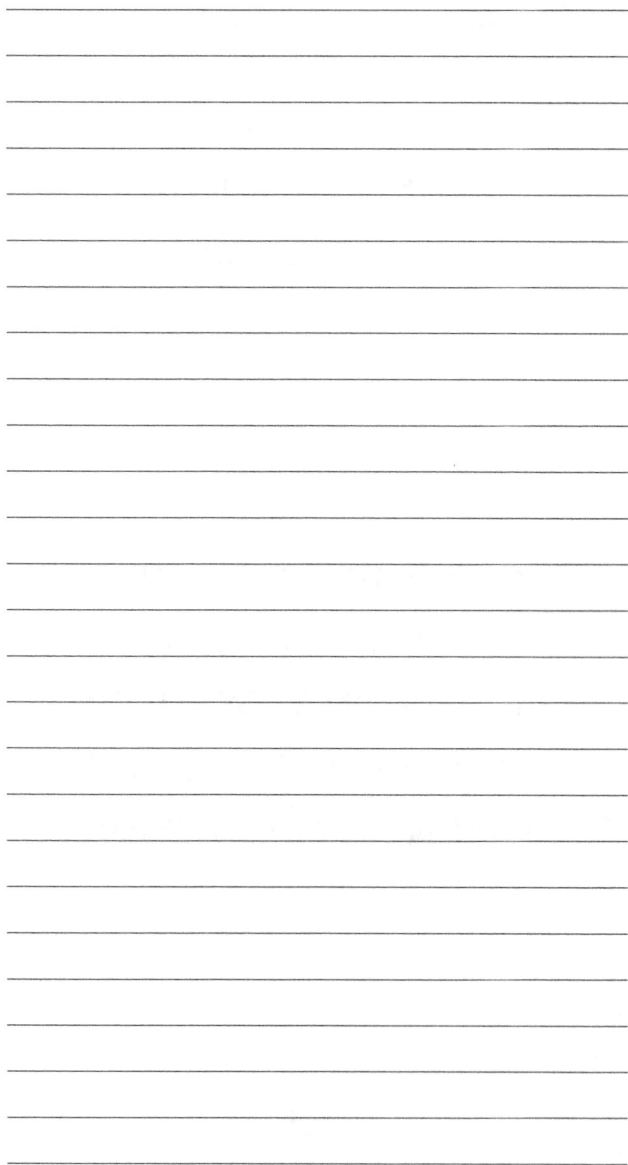

IF ONLY MY MOTHER
HAD TOLD ME...

EVERYTHING IS POSSIBLE:
DON'T RULE OUT
ANY OPTION, WHATSOEVER,
UNTIL IT'S CLEAR TO YOU
THAT IT'S NOT AN OPTION.

#19

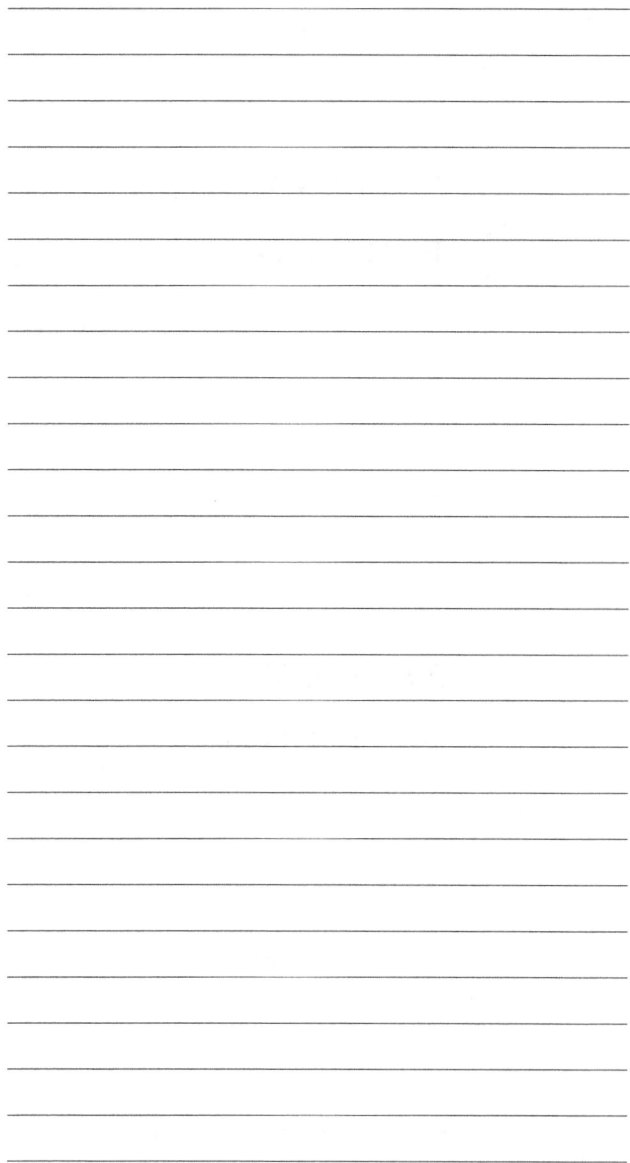

IF ONLY MY MOTHER
HAD TOLD ME...

YOU ARE BEAUTY,
NOTHING LESS.

#20

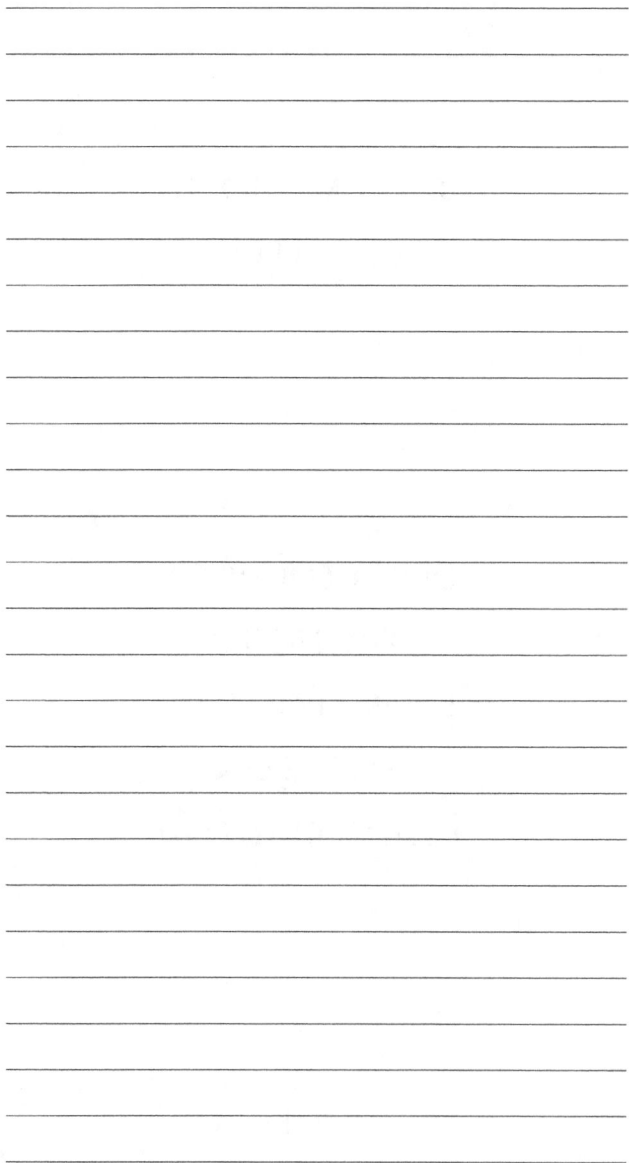

IF ONLY MY MOTHER
HAD TOLD ME...

DON'T FOCUS ON
TRYING TO
LOOK BEAUTIFUL;
FOCUS ON
FEELING BEAUTIFUL.

#21

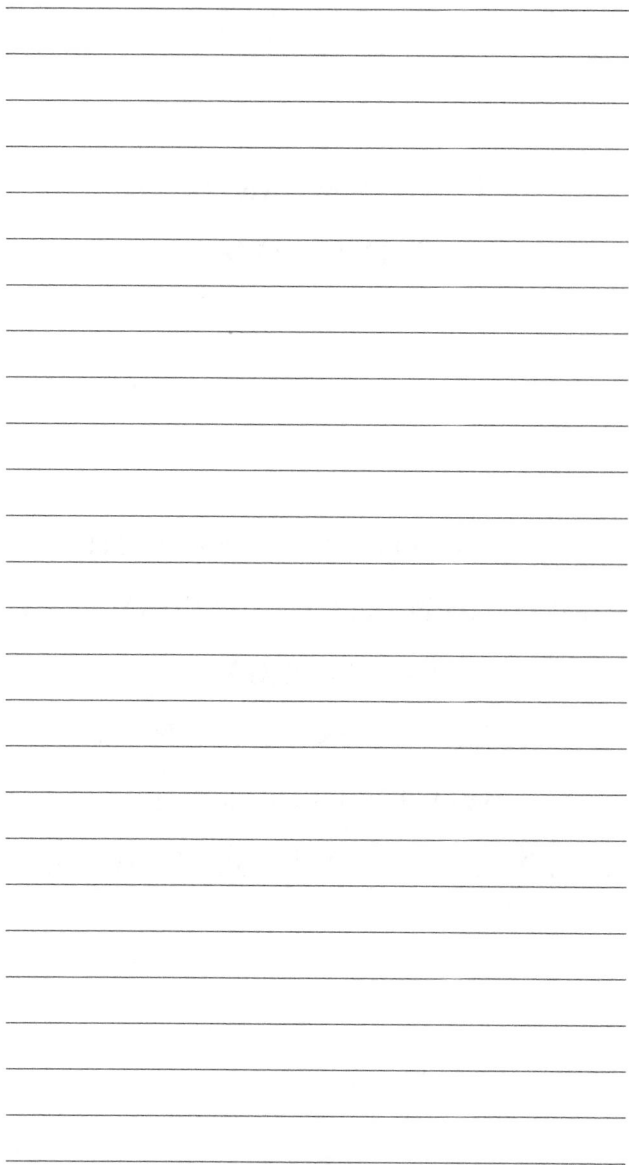

IF ONLY MY MOTHER
HAD TOLD ME...

LAUGHTER IS ONE OF THE
MOST IMPORTANT INGREDIENTS
IN A MARRIAGE.
IF YOU AREN'T LAUGHING
WITH YOUR PARTNER,
SOMETHING HAS GONE AWRY.

#22

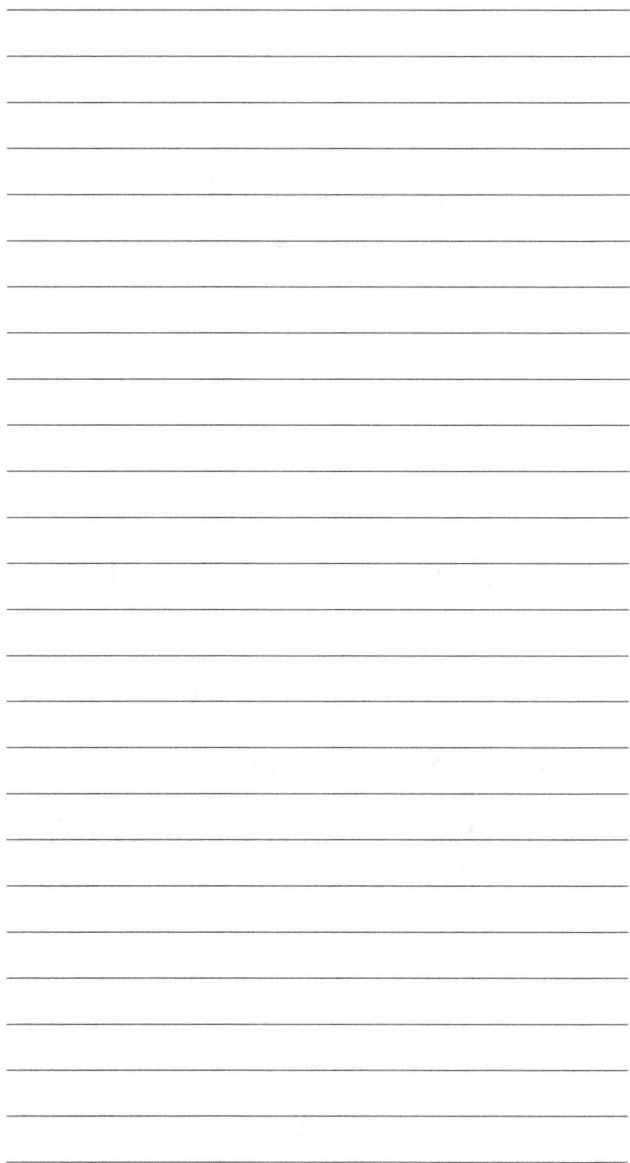

IF ONLY MY MOTHER
HAD TOLD ME...

CHILDREN ARE A LIFE-LONG
COMMITMENT;
YOU WILL NEVER STOP
WANTING TO PROTECT THEM
OR MAKE THEIR PAIN GO AWAY.

#23

IF ONLY MY MOTHER
HAD TOLD ME...

ANGELS ARE REALLY REAL,
& WE NEED TO LISTEN TO THEM
EVERY SINGLE MINUTE OF THE DAY.

#24

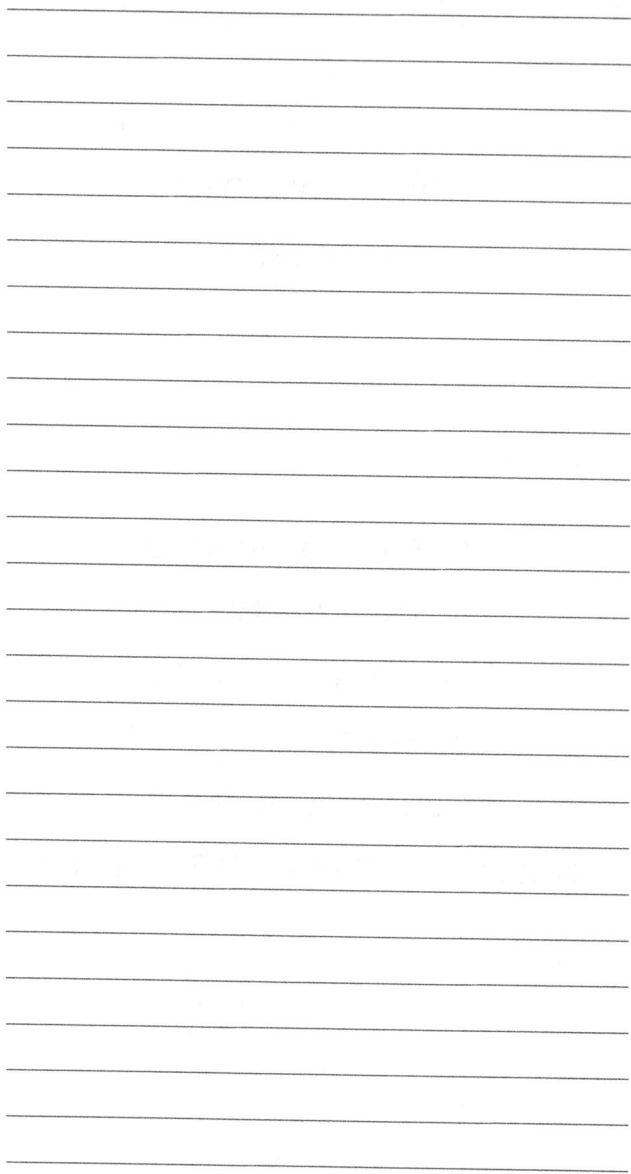

IF ONLY MY MOTHER
HAD TOLD ME...

WE GET IN TROUBLE
IN OUR LIVES
WHEN WE FORGET
THAT WE ARE, AFTER ALL,
SPIRITUAL BEINGS
HAVING A HUMAN EXPERIENCE.

#25

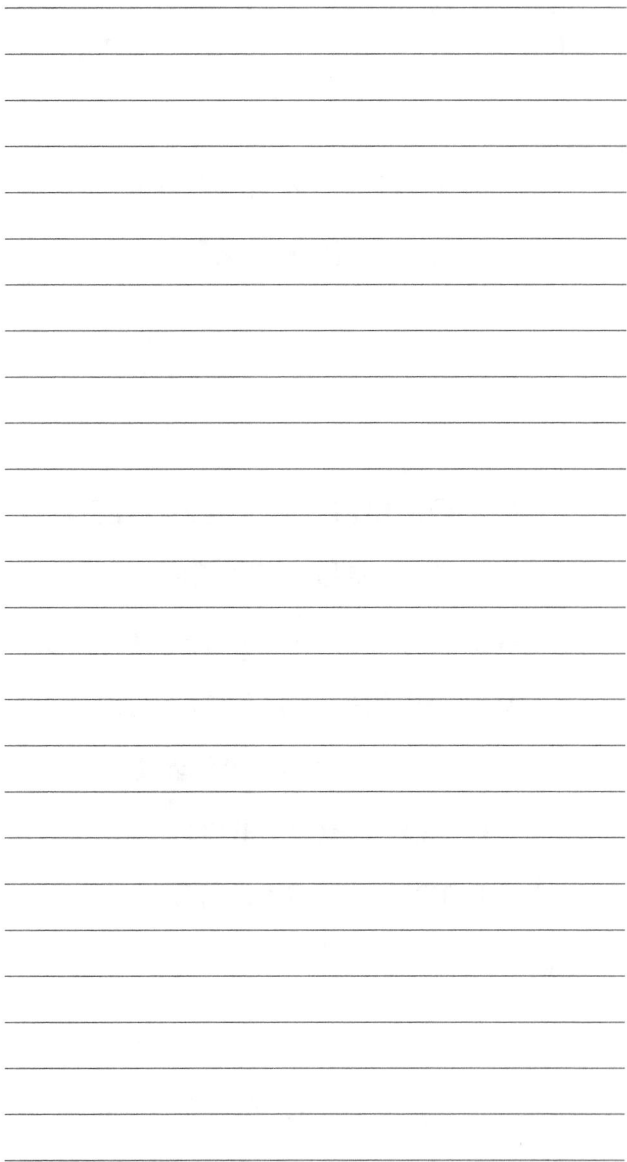

IF ONLY MY MOTHER
HAD TOLD ME...

MAJOR LIFE CHALLENGES
DON'T MEAN THERE IS
SOMETHING WRONG WITH US.
MAJOR LIFE CHALLENGES
ARE HERE TO GROW US
INTO WHOLE BEINGS,
BODY, HEART & SOUL.

#26

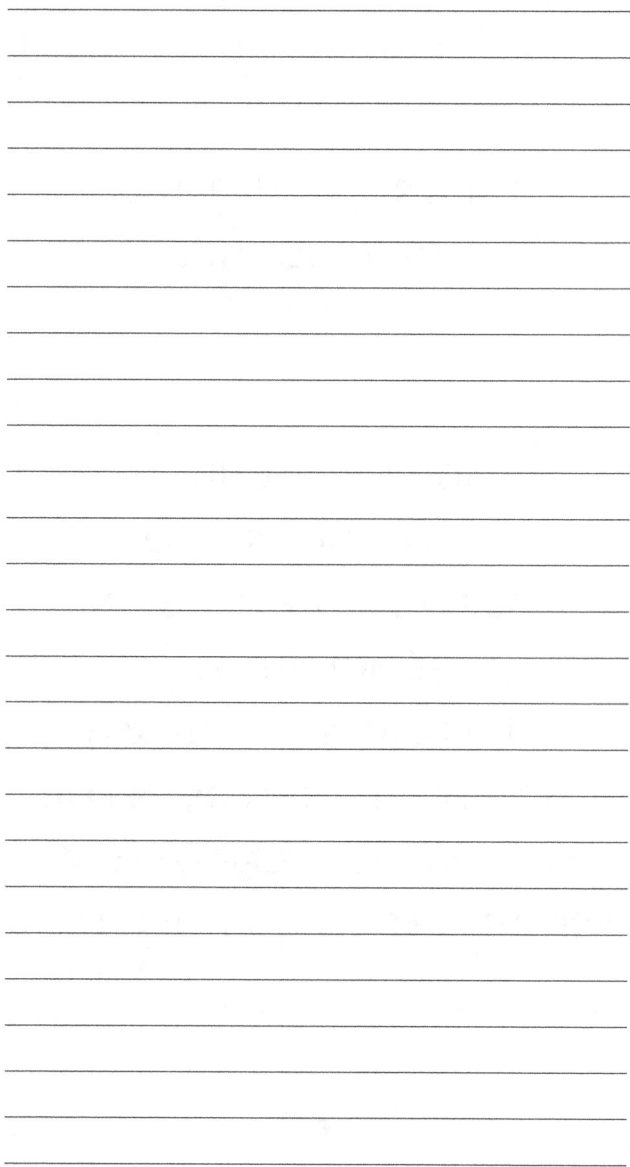

IF ONLY MY MOTHER
HAD TOLD ME...

AGING IS REQUIRED
TO BRING US INTO
OUR FULLEST EXPRESSION.
THE MOMENT THAT
THE BLUSH IS OFF THE ROSE,
IS THE BEGINNING OF AN EPIC
JOURNEY THAT CAN ONLY BE
EXPERIENCED TO BE UNDERSTOOD.

#27

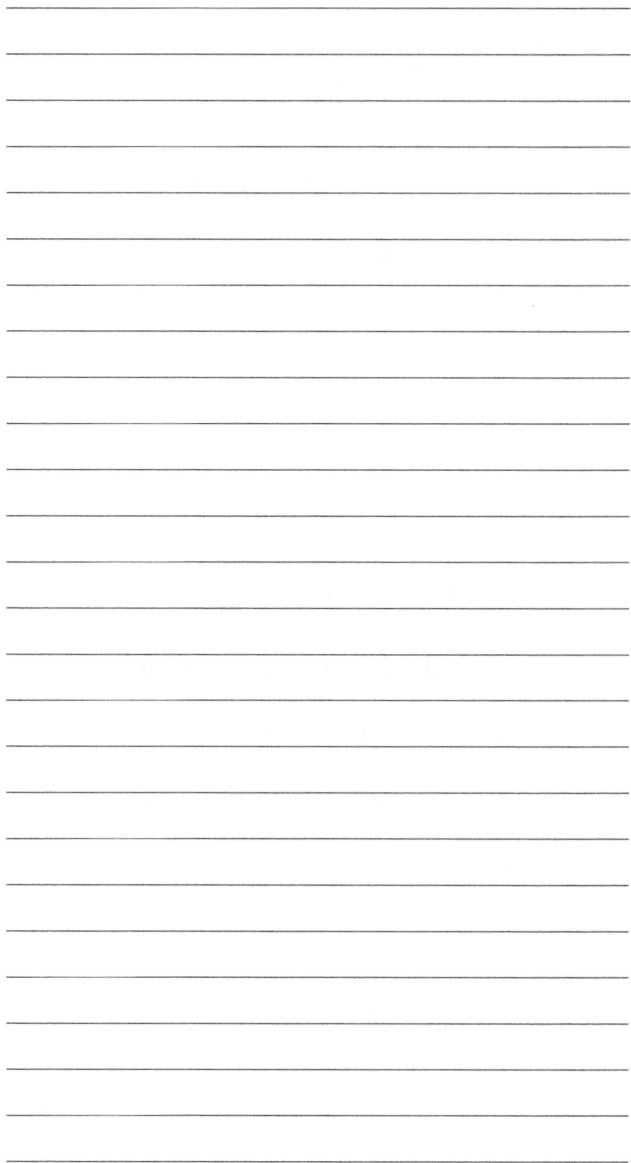

IF ONLY MY MOTHER
HAD TOLD ME...

THERE IS NO
HAPPILY EVER AFTER.
BUT THERE IS
HAPPIER EVER AFTER.

#28

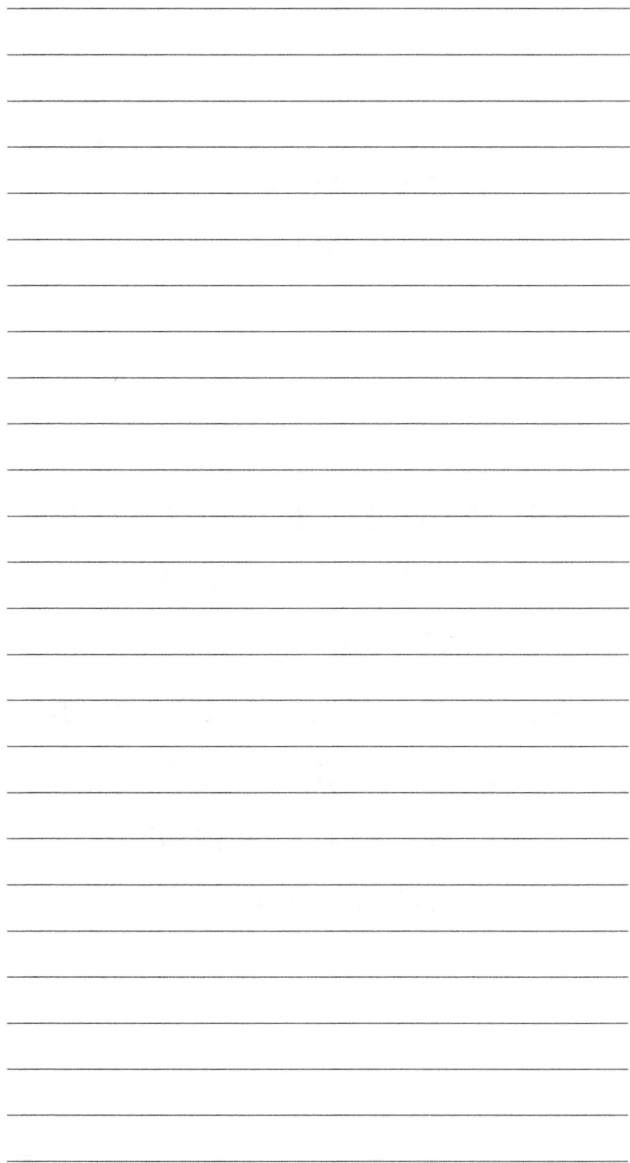

IF ONLY MY MOTHER
HAD TOLD ME...

YOU ARE ENTITLED TO CREATE &
HAVE FOR YOURSELF,
AS MUCH HAPPINESS & LOVE
AS HUMANLY POSSIBLE FOR YOU.
YOU'RE NOT ENTITLED
TO HAVE OTHER PEOPLE
MANIFEST UP FOR YOU.

#29

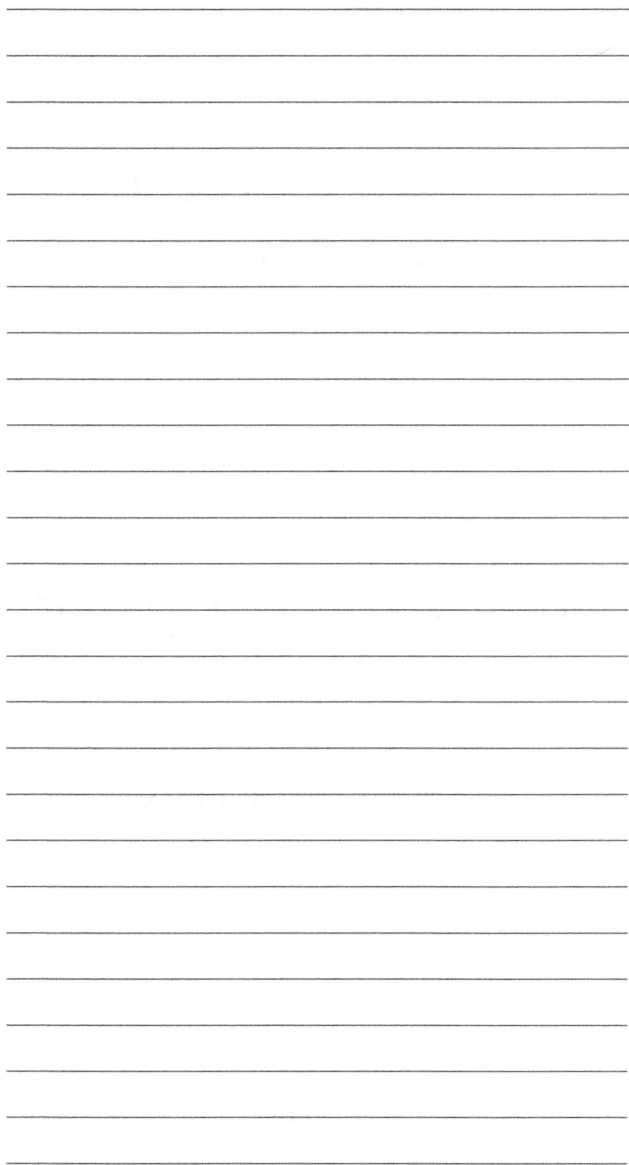

IF ONLY MY MOTHER
HAD TOLD ME...

MONEY DOESN'T MAKE YOUR LIFE
BETTER, SAFER,
MORE SECURE;
IT'S JUST FUN TO HAVE.

#30

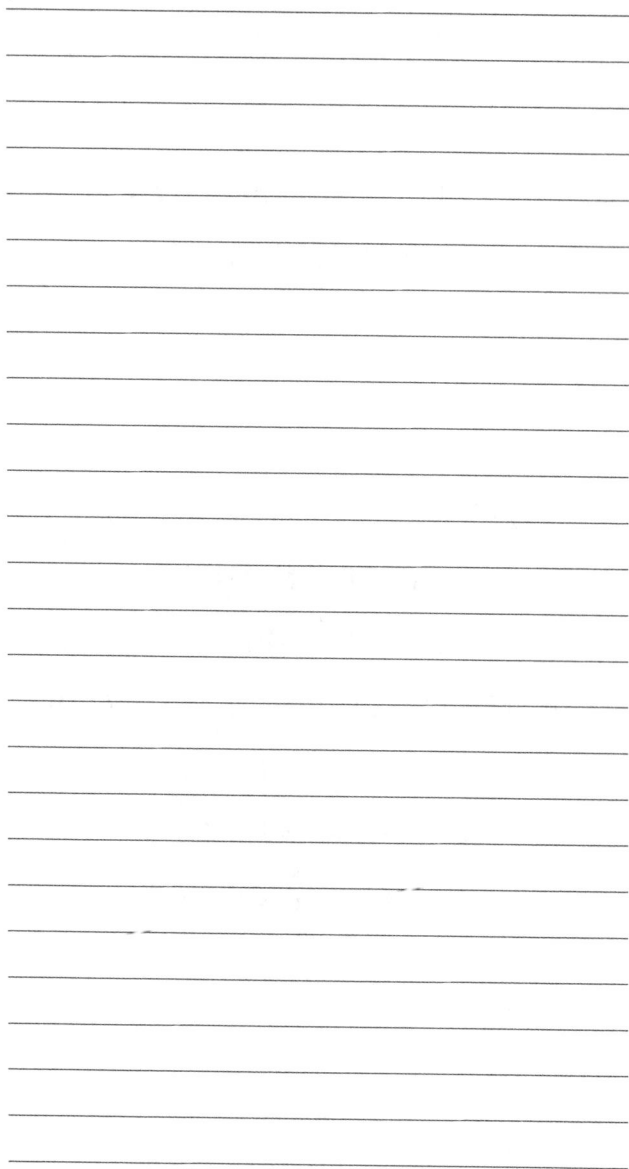

IF ONLY MY MOTHER
HAD TOLD ME...

OTHER PEOPLE'S LIVES LOOK
EASIER, SHINIER,
MORE PROSPEROUS.
TO THEM, YOUR LIFE MAY LOOK
EASIER, SHINIER &
MORE PROSPEROUS.
WE CAN'T KNOW.

#31

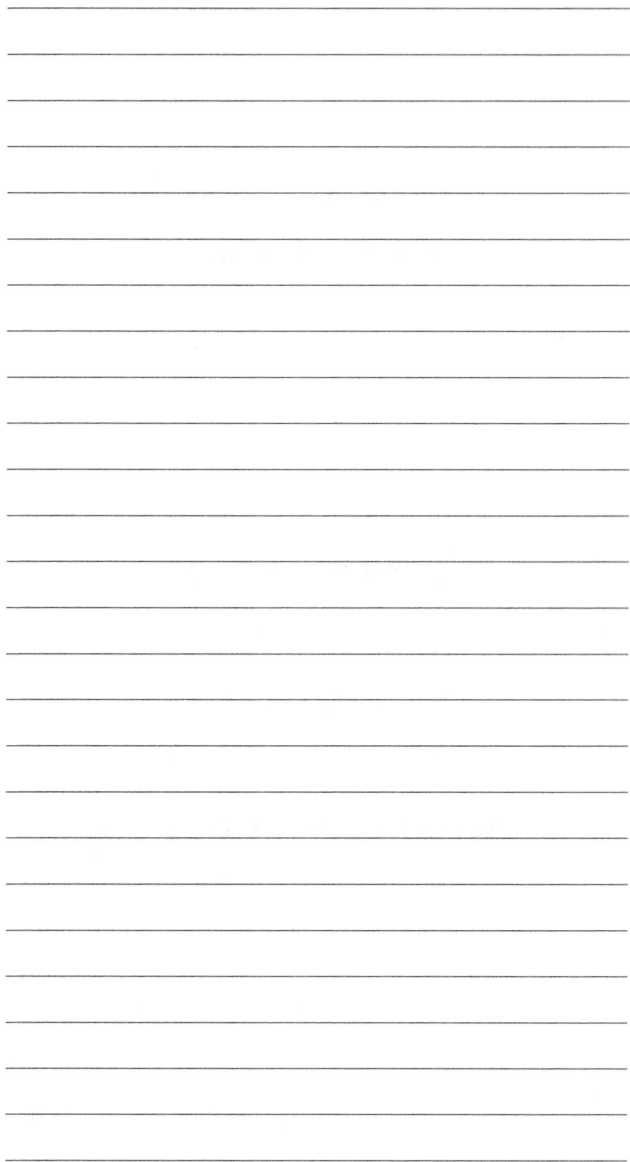

IF ONLY MY MOTHER
HAD TOLD ME...

COMPARING YOURSELF
TO OTHERS
WILL CAUSE YOU
TO LOSE SIGHT OF
WHAT'S YOURS TO DO.

#32

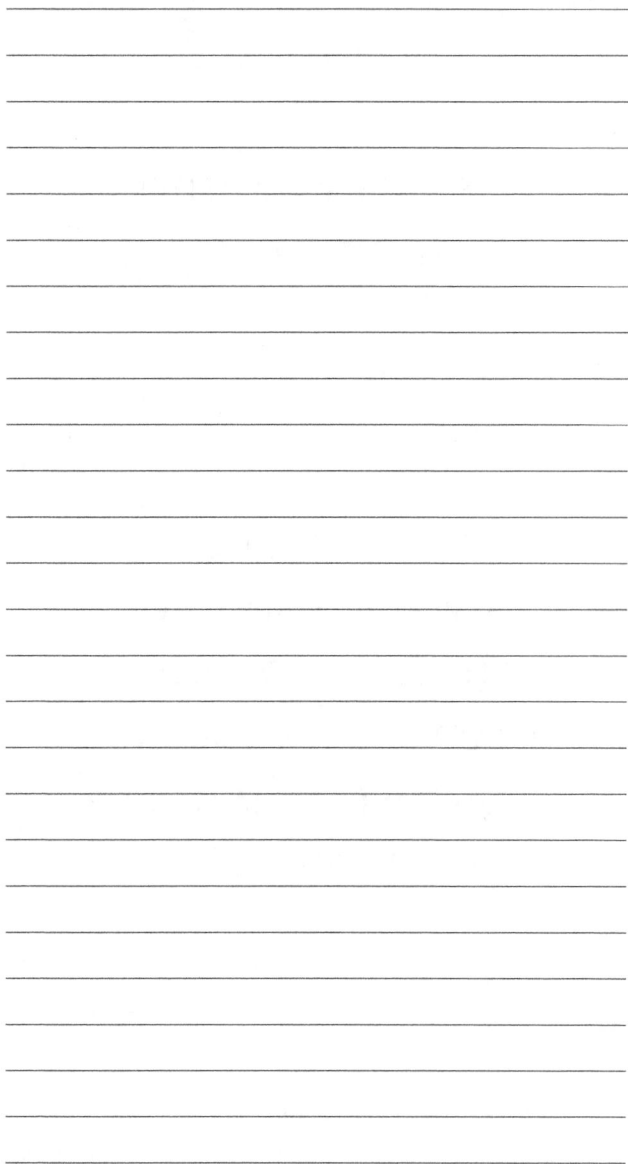

IF ONLY MY MOTHER
HAD TOLD ME...

THERE IS NO
OWNER'S MANUAL OR
BLUEPRINT TO FOLLOW,
(THAT WE CAN SEE, ANYWAY).
YOU HAVE TO MAKE IT UP
AS YOU GO.

#33

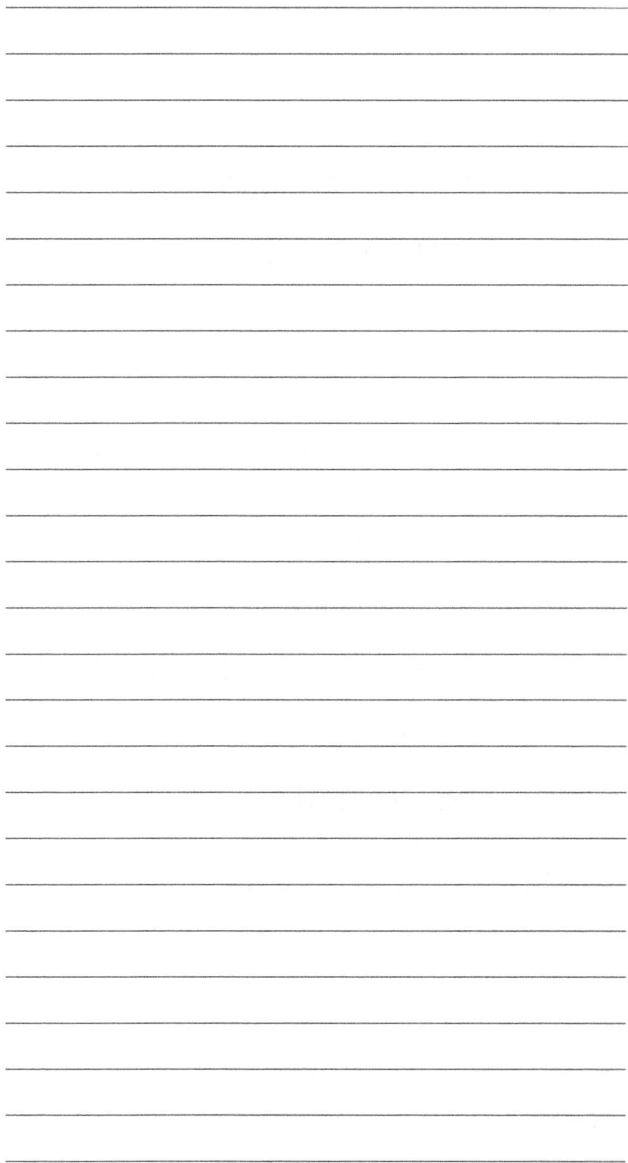

IF ONLY MY MOTHER
HAD TOLD ME...

THERE REALLY
ISN'T A BETTER LIFE;
THERE IS ONLY
A DIFFERENT LIFE.

#34

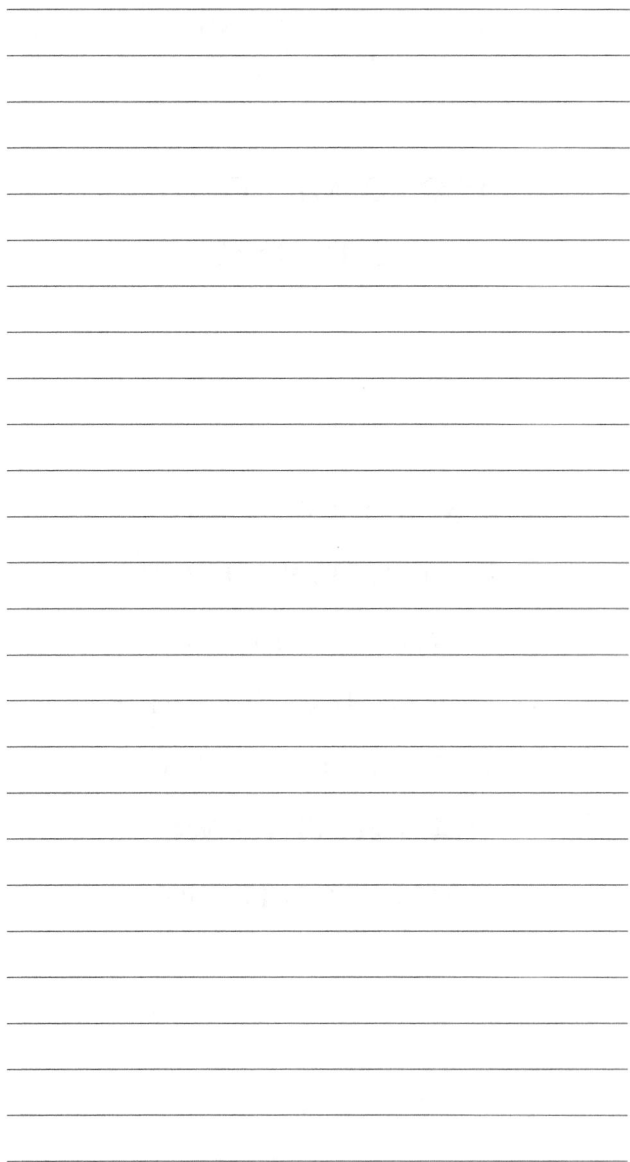

IF ONLY MY MOTHER
HAD TOLD ME...

IT'S NOT A BAD THING
TO DESIRE, TO WISH & WANT
WHAT YOU WANT.
YOU JUST HAVE TO DETACH
FROM THE IDEA THAT
HAVING THEM WILL
MAKE YOU HAPPY.

#35

IF ONLY MY MOTHER
HAD TOLD ME...

WE START OUT WITH TONS
OF MEMORY – MOST OF WHICH
IS UNCONSCIOUS.
THE PRACTICE IS TO CHOOSE
WHICH MEMORIES ARE
BASED ON TRUTHS, & WHICH
ARE BASED ON FEAR.

#36

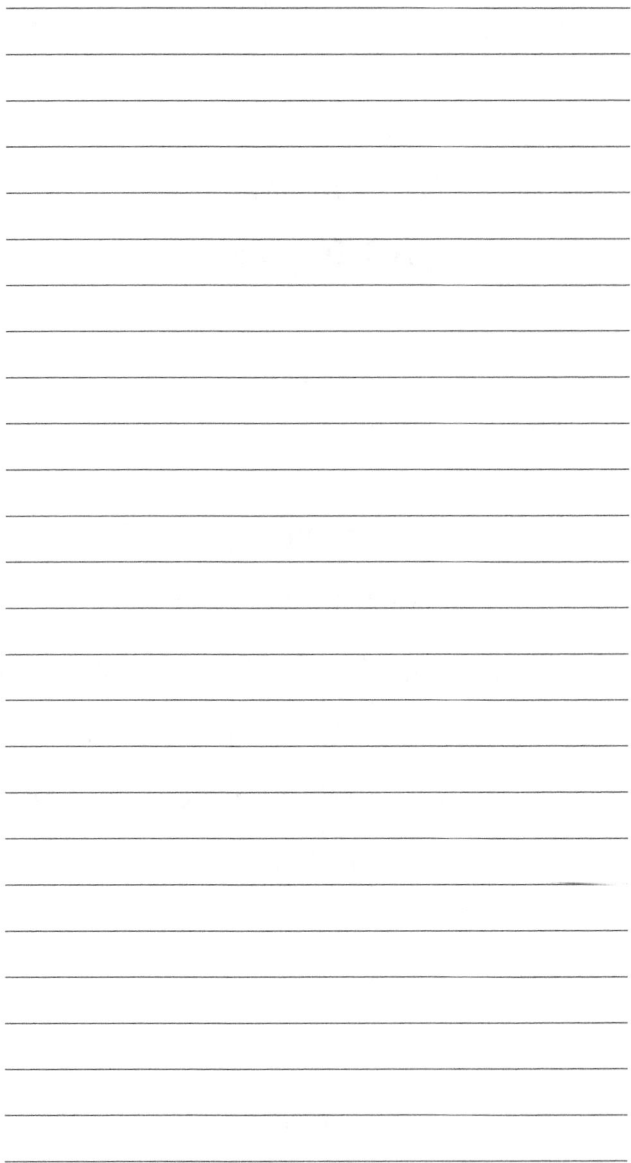

IF ONLY MY MOTHER
HAD TOLD ME...

JUST BECAUSE
IT HAPPENED ONCE,
IT DOESN'T MEAN YOU HAVE
TO LIVE YOUR WHOLE LIFE
AS IF IT'S GOING
TO HAPPEN AGAIN.

#37

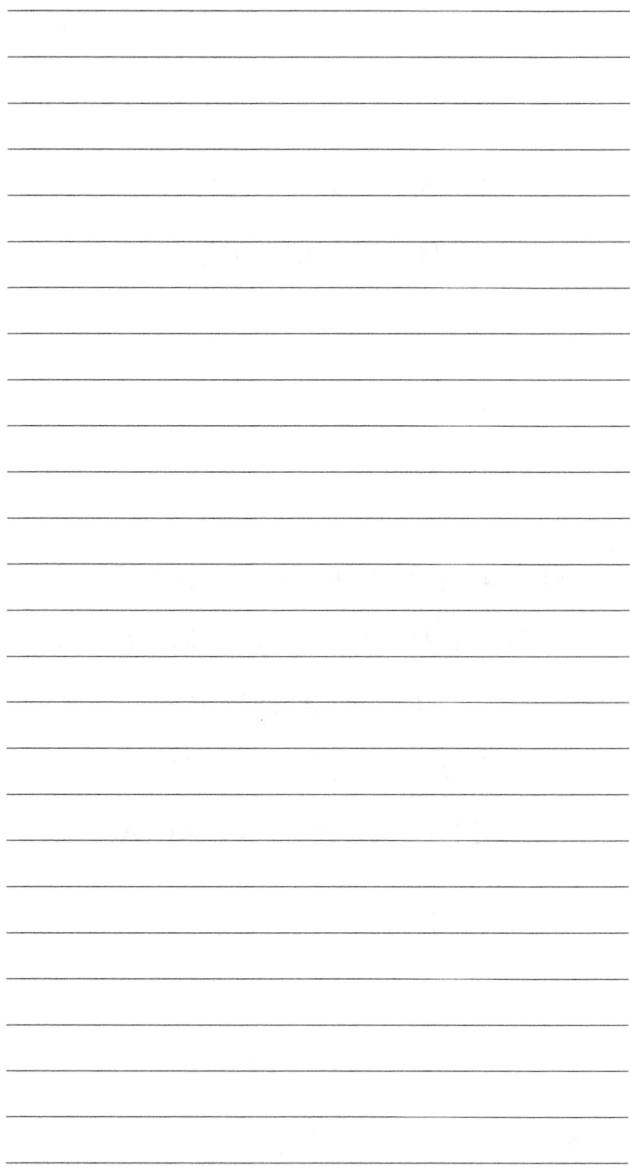

IF ONLY MY MOTHER
HAD TOLD ME...

HONOR YOUR TRUE NATURE –
THAT'S WHAT YOU CAME HERE
TO DO ANYWAY,
SO YOU MIGHT AS WELL
BEGIN DOING IT NOW.

#38

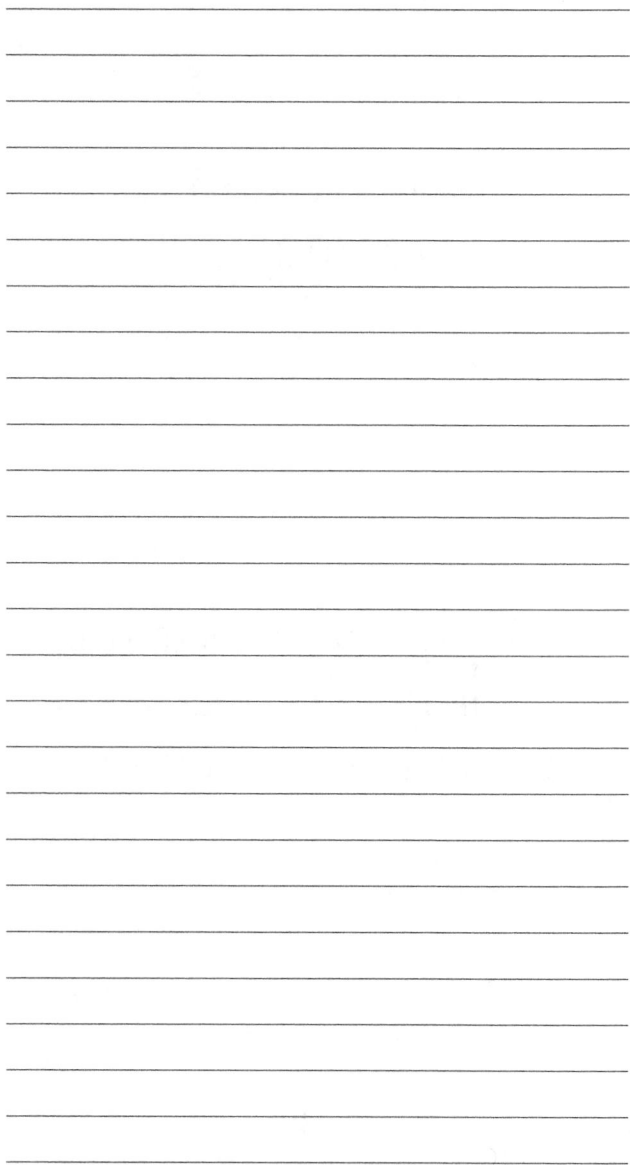

IF ONLY MY MOTHER
HAD TOLD ME...

PRACTICE BEING GRATEFUL
FOR THE WAY THAT IT IS
& FOR THE WAY THAT IT ISN'T.

#39

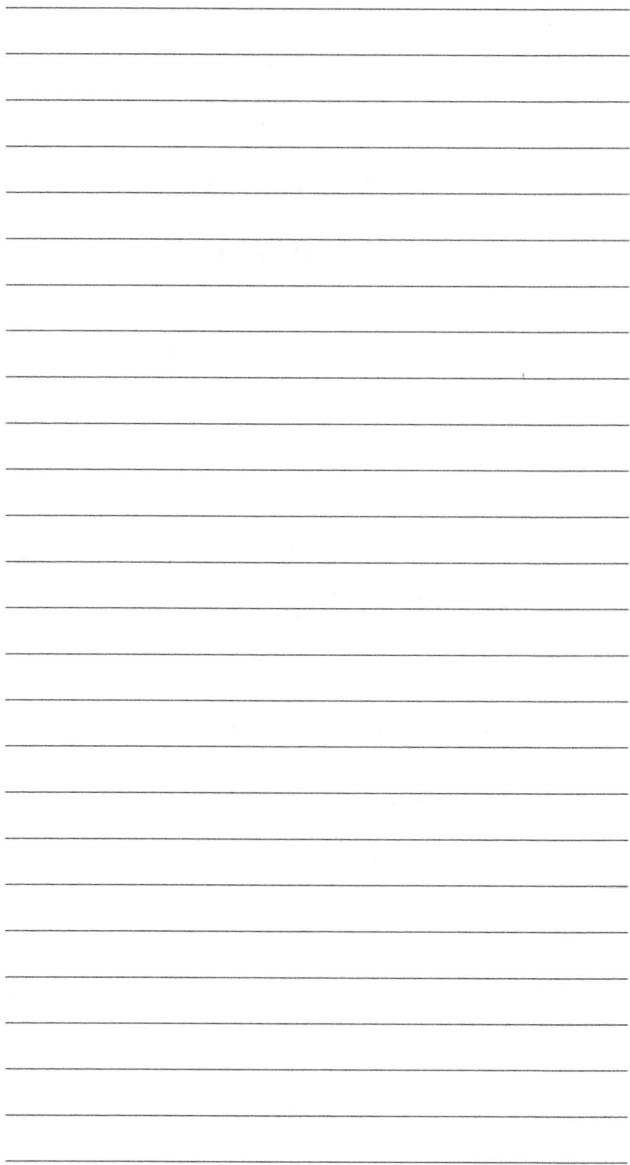

IF ONLY MY MOTHER
HAD TOLD ME...

WHEN LIFE GETS HARD,
IT'S EASY TO FORGET
THAT YOU ARE THE ETERNAL
PRESENCE OF DIVINE GRACE.

#40

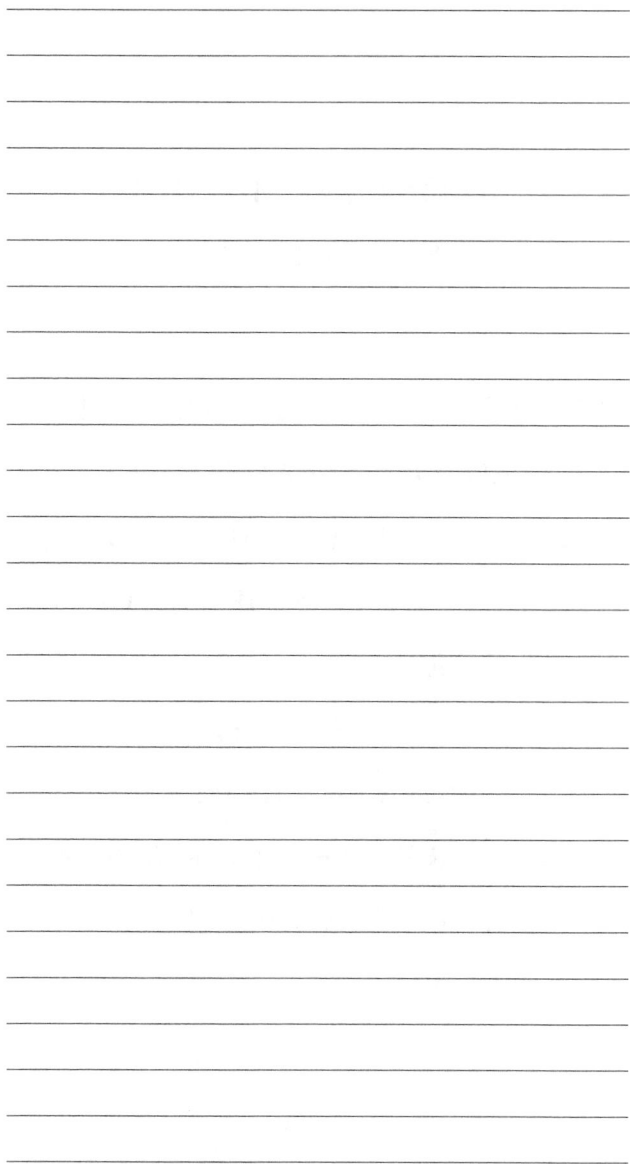

IF ONLY MY MOTHER
HAD TOLD ME...

YOU ARE LIMITLESS POTENTIALITY.
ANYONE OR ANYTHING
THAT LIMITS YOU, IN ANY WAY,
IS PROVIDING AN OPPORTUNITY
FOR YOU TO DISCERN
YOUR TRUTH,
YOUR COMMITMENTS
& YOUR FULLEST EXPRESSION
OF YOUR ESSENTIAL SELF.

#41

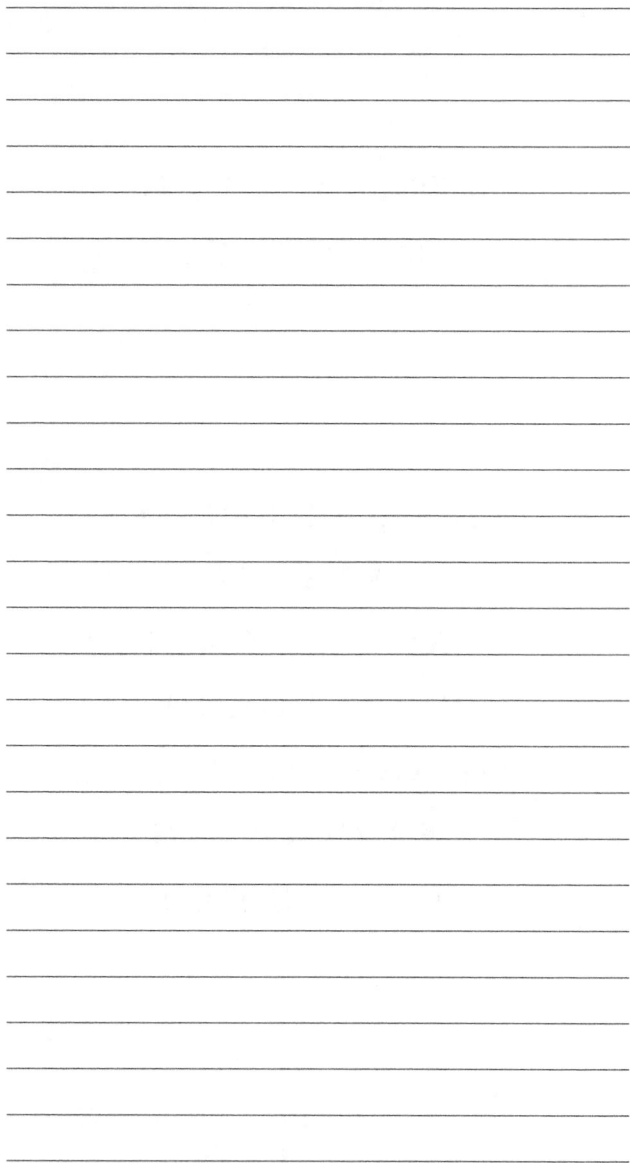

IF ONLY MY MOTHER
HAD TOLD ME...

DIS-EASE IS CAUSED
BY A BELIEF
THAT YOU LACK SOMETHING
IN THIS MOMENT,
& SELF-LOVE IS THE PRACTICE
OF REMEMBERING
YOU LACK NOTHING.

#42

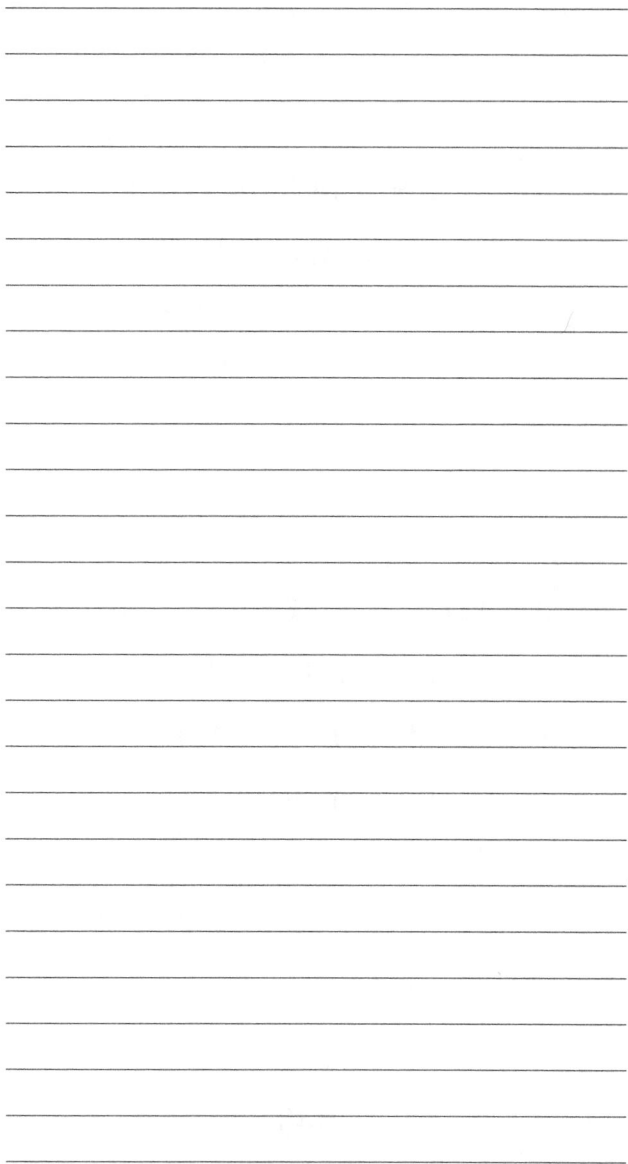

IF ONLY MY MOTHER
HAD TOLD ME...

LET ALL YOUR FEELINGS OUT –
FEEL THEM ALL!
THAT'S WHAT WE CAME HERE
TO EXPERIENCE.

#43

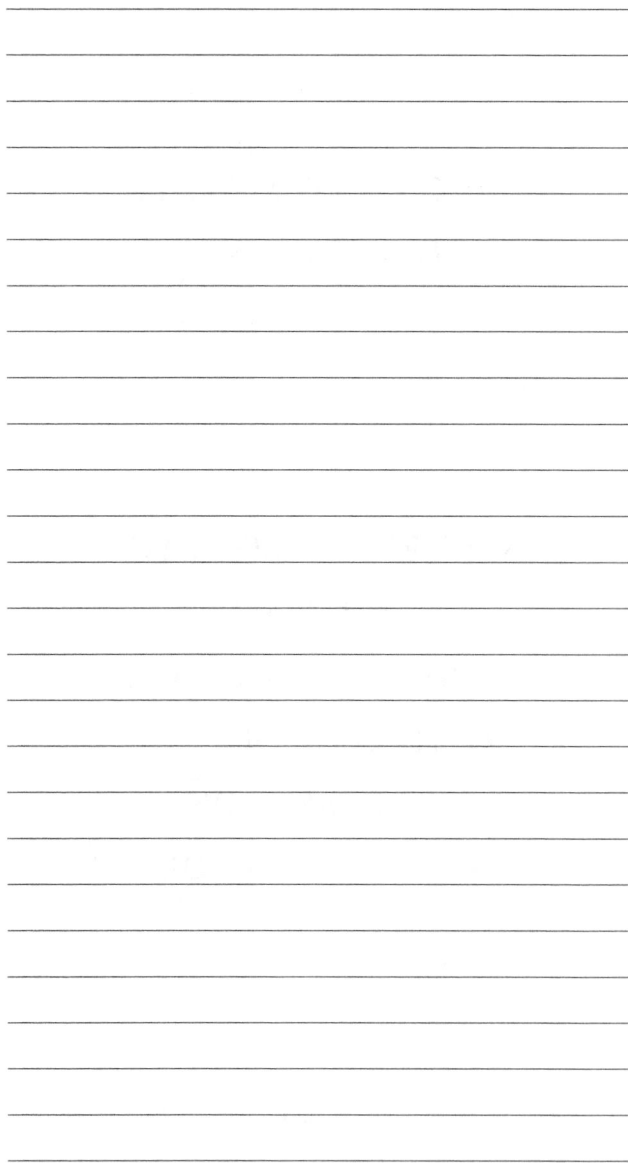

IF ONLY MY MOTHER
HAD TOLD ME...

BE CURIOUS ABOUT YOU!
AFTER ALL,
YOUR RELATIONSHIPS
WITH EVERYONE ELSE
ARE BASED ON
WHO YOU THINK YOU ARE.

#44

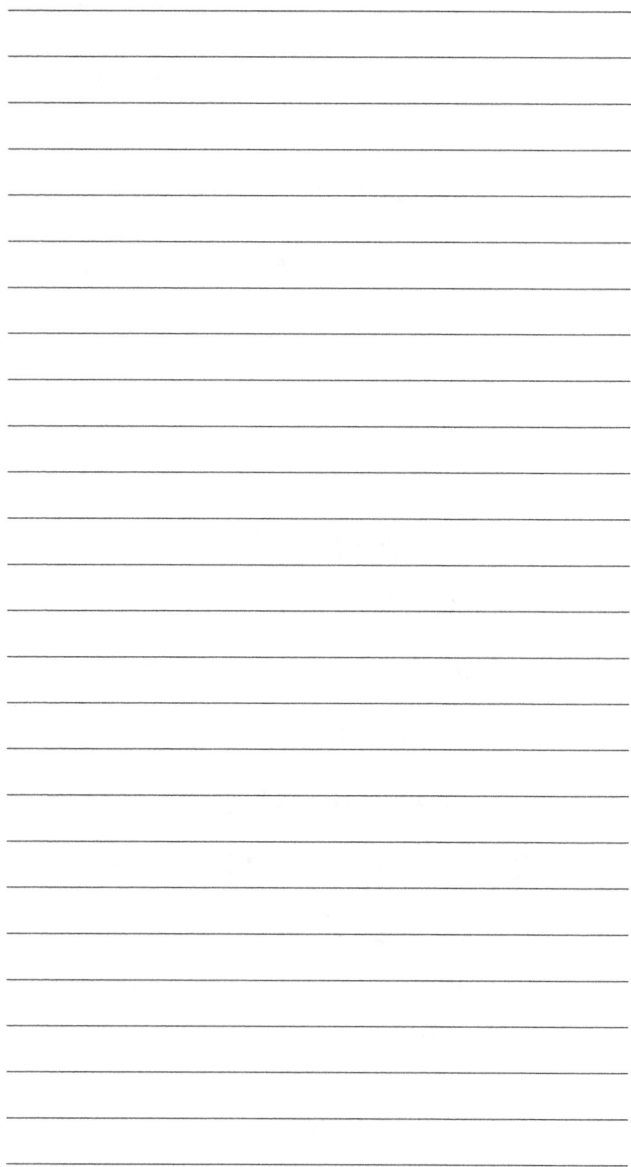

IF ONLY MY MOTHER
HAD TOLD ME...

IN EVERY LIFE ENDEAVOR,
PRACTICE IS ESSENTIAL
TO BRING ABOUT MASTERY.
THERE IS NO UGLY,
BAD OR FAILURE;
THERE IS ONLY THE NEXT
LEVEL OF MASTERY.

#45

IF ONLY MY MOTHER
HAD TOLD ME...

FIRST, GIVE YOURSELF
PERMISSION
TO DO/HAVE/BE
WHATEVER YOU WANT.
THIS WILL LEAD YOU
TO WHAT'S NEXT.

#46

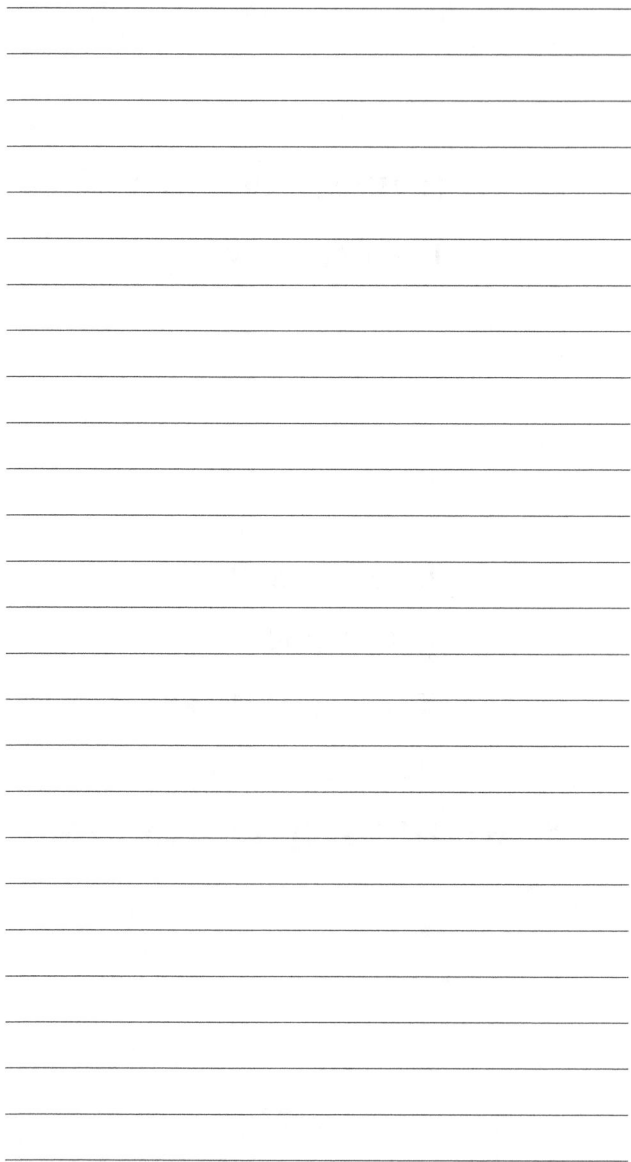

IF ONLY MY MOTHER

HAD TOLD ME...

LIFE IS A SERIES

OF INTERNSHIPS.

EVEN THE MASTERS

ARE LEARNING

SOMETHING NEW EVERY DAY.

#47

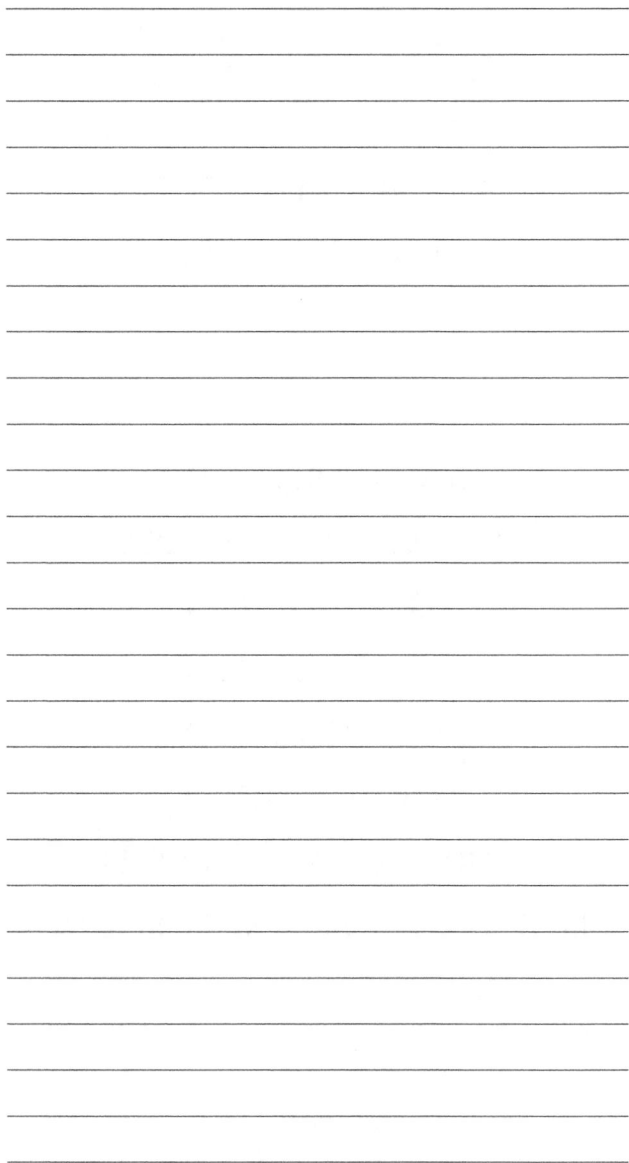

IF ONLY MY MOTHER
HAD TOLD ME...

GIVE UP BELIEVING
THAT YOU ARE SUPPOSED
TO GET IT RIGHT
THE FIRST TIME,
THE SECOND TIME
OR THE THIRD.
RARELY DO WE LEAP TALL
BUILDINGS IN A SINGLE BOUND.

#48

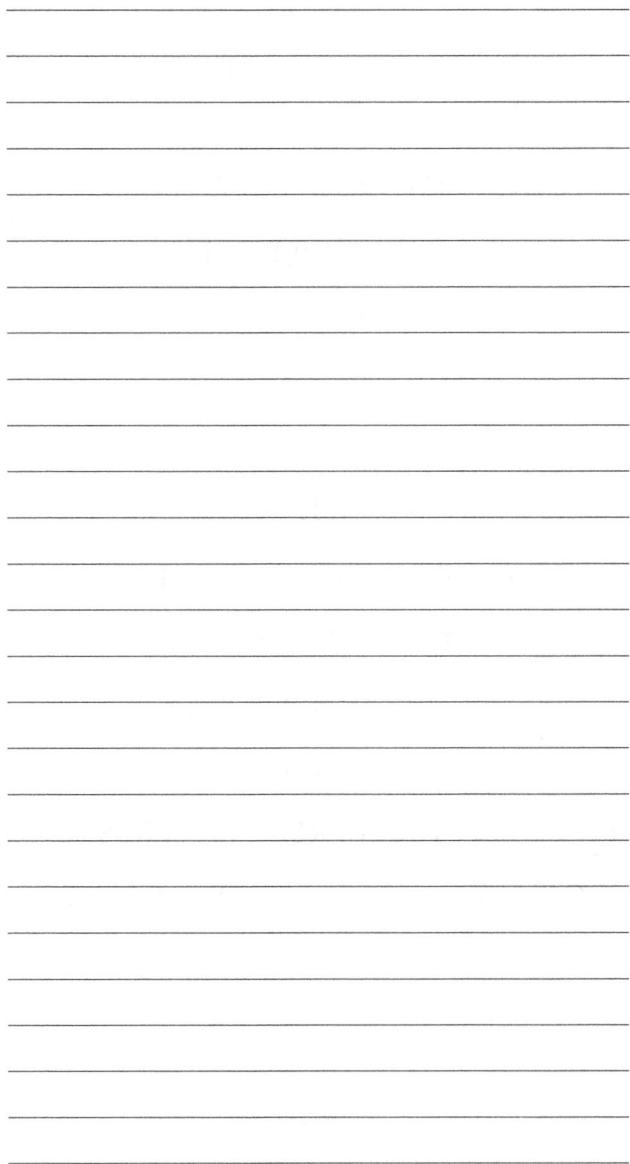

IF ONLY MY MOTHER
HAD TOLD ME...

RELATIONSHIPS ARE ONLY
MEANT TO GROW US INTO
HIGHER LEVELS OF
CONSCIOUSNESS.
THEY ARE NOT MEANT TO
RESCUE US FROM DISTRESS,
OR HAVE US FEEL SAFE & SECURE.

#49

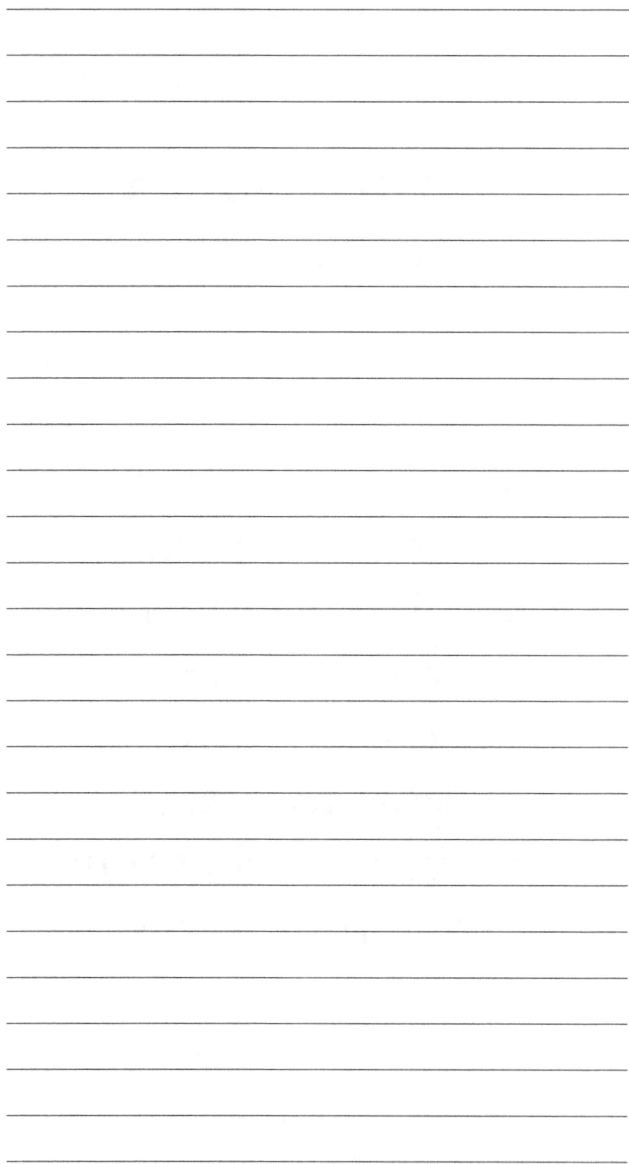

IF ONLY MY MOTHER
HAD TOLD ME...

WHEN YOU STOP GROWING
IN A RELATIONSHIP,
YOU EITHER HAVE SOMETHING
MORE TO LEARN,
OR YOU HAVE NOTHING
MORE TO LEARN.
ONLY YOU CAN FIGURE OUT
WHICH ONE IS TRUE.

#50

IF ONLY MY MOTHER
HAD TOLD ME...

YOU CAN'T AVOID
EXPERIENCING
ANY EMOTION
THAT IS PART OF THE
HUMAN EXPERIENCE,
UNTIL YOU STOP BEING HUMAN.

#51

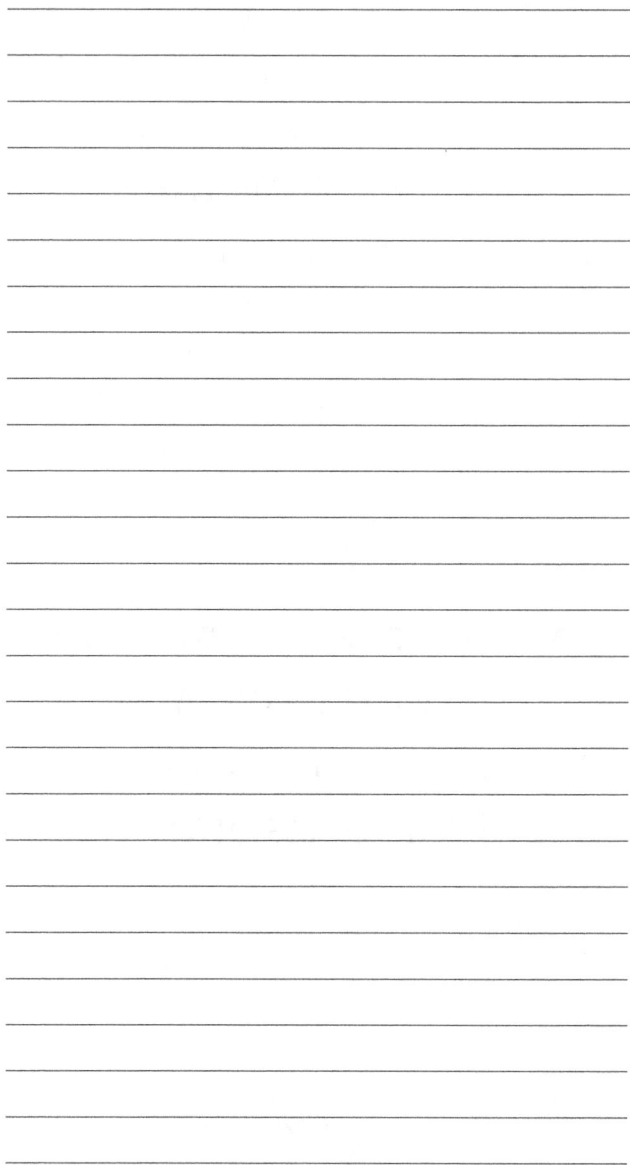

IF ONLY MY MOTHER
HAD TOLD ME...

DEATH IS THE FINAL FRONTIER.
THE PROCESS OF DYING
CAN BE AS ADVENTUROUS
AS THE PROCESS OF LIVING.

#52

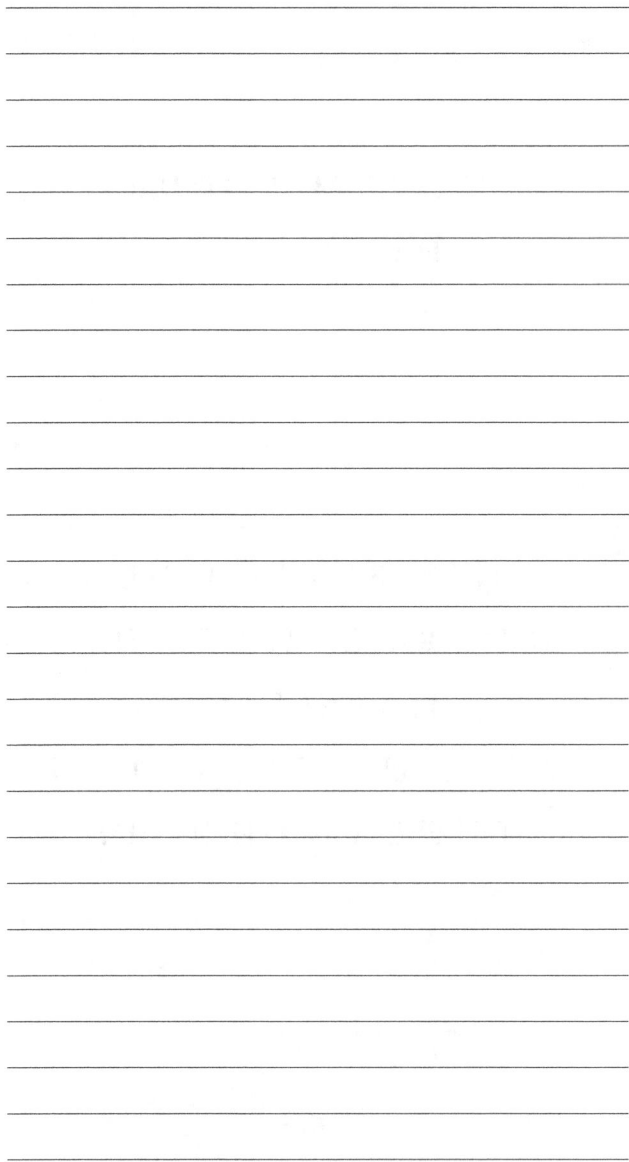

IF ONLY MY MOTHER
HAD TOLD ME...

NO MATTER HOW OLD
YOU LOOK ON THE OUTSIDE,
IT MOST LIKELY
WON'T REFLECT HOW YOUNG
YOU FEEL ON THE INSIDE.

#53

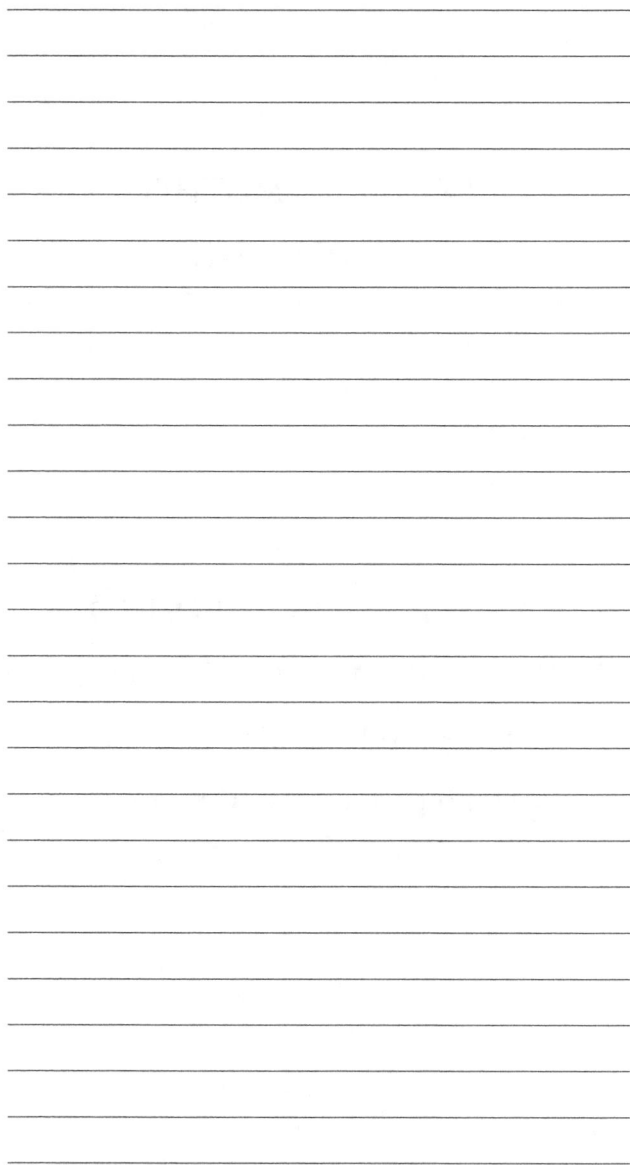

IF ONLY MY MOTHER
HAD TOLD ME...

STOP HANGING AROUND
PEOPLE WHO DO NOT HONOR YOU
& TREAT YOU WITH RESPECT.
IT ISN'T GOOD FOR YOU.

#54

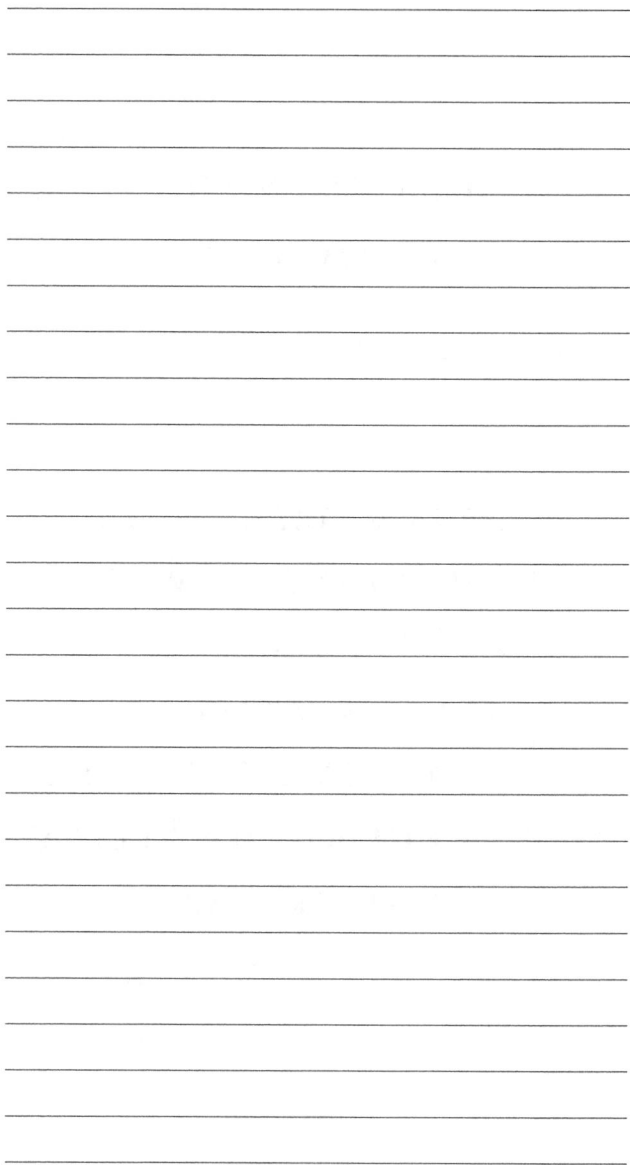

IF ONLY MY MOTHER
HAD TOLD ME...

DON'T MARRY A PERSON
IF THEY DO NOT VIEW YOU
WITH THE UTMOST LOVE,
RESPECT & ACCEPTANCE,
& THEY DON'T VIEW THEMSELVES
WITH THE UTMOST LOVE, RESPECT
& ACCEPTANCE.

#55

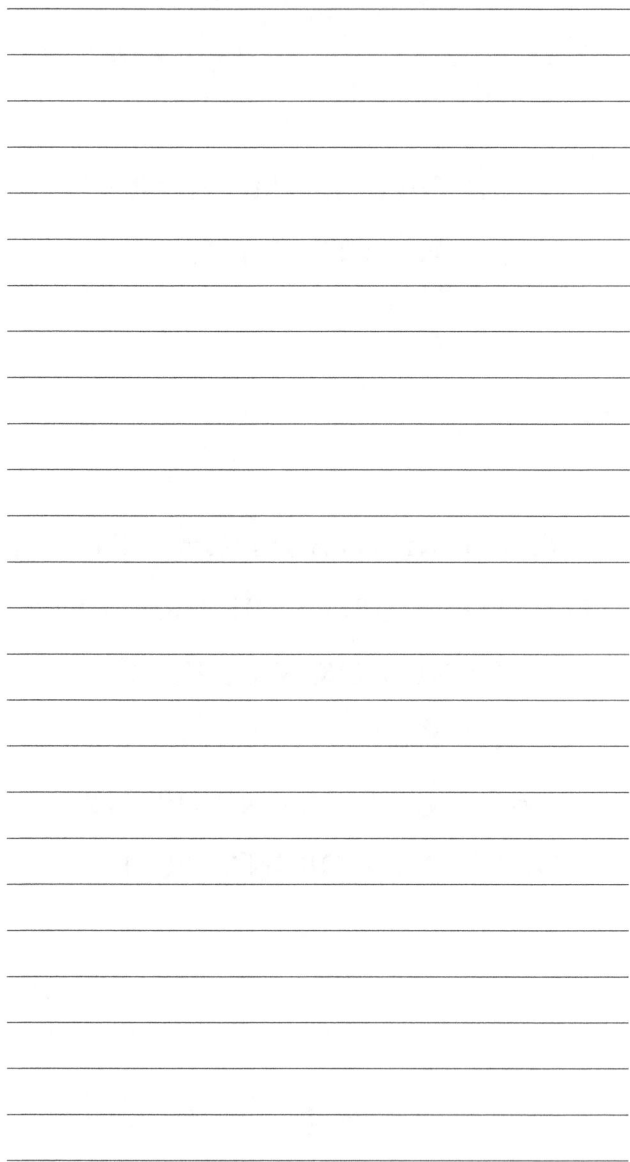

IF ONLY MY MOTHER
HAD TOLD ME...

IT'S OKAY TO ACKNOWLEDGE
OTHER PEOPLE'S DIFFERENCES.
IT'S NOT OKAY TO JUDGE
THOSE DIFFERENCES AS
WRONG, BAD, UNWORTHY,
UNLOVABLE OR INADEQUATE.

#56

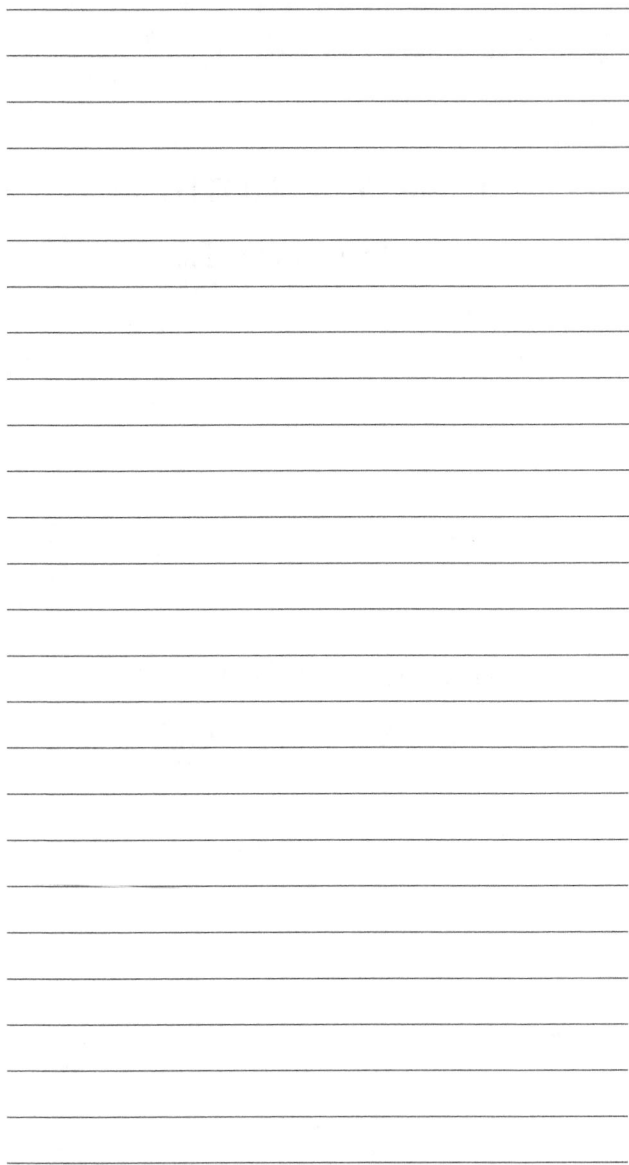

IF ONLY MY MOTHER
HAD TOLD ME...

IF IT ISN'T A HELL YES,
IT'S A HELL NO!

#57

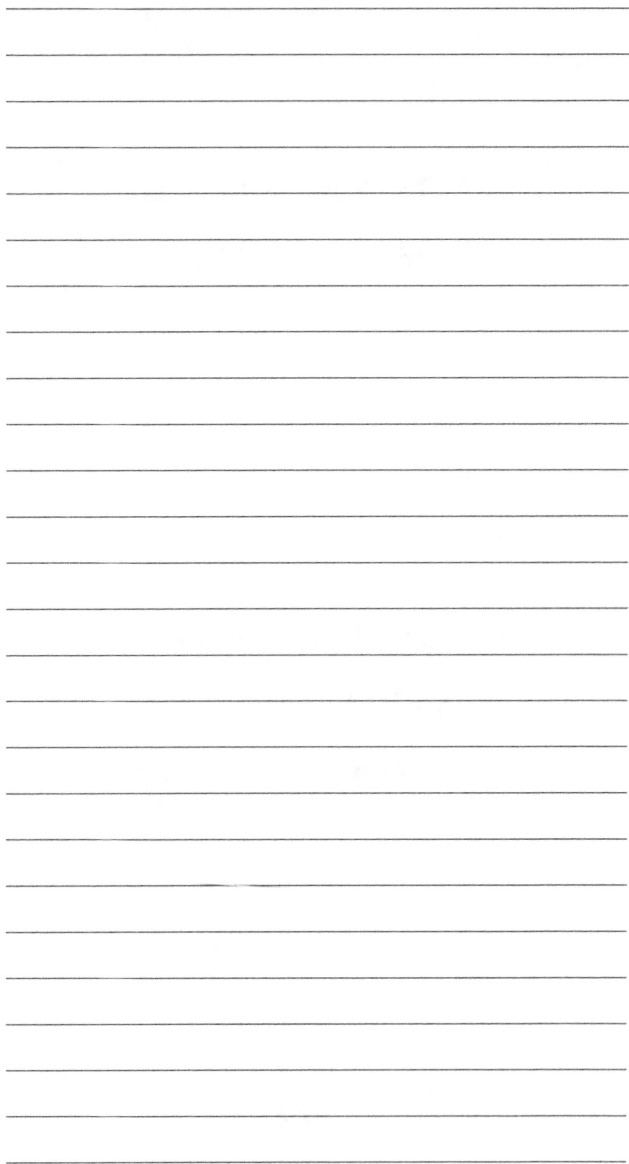

IF ONLY MY MOTHER
HAD TOLD ME...

LIVING INTO THE UNKNOWN
IS WHAT ALL OF US
DO EVERY SINGLE DAY.

#58

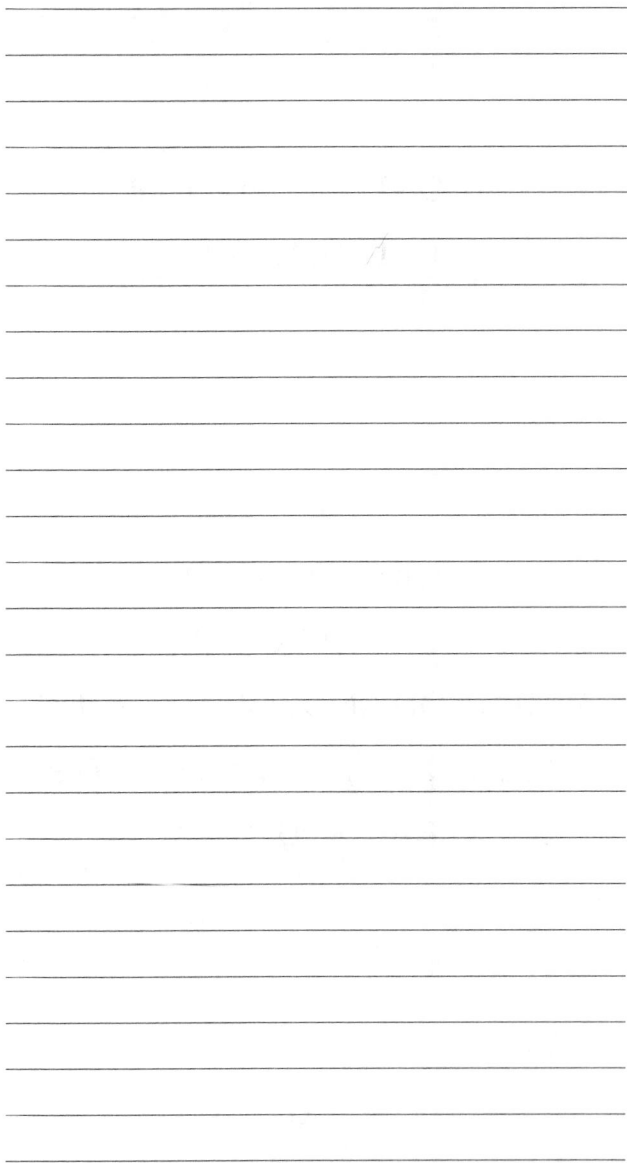

IF ONLY MY MOTHER
HAD TOLD ME...

YOU WILL KNOW
WHAT TO DO
WHEN YOU KNOW WHAT TO DO.
YOU CAN'T KNOW ANY FASTER
THAN YOU KNOW.

#59

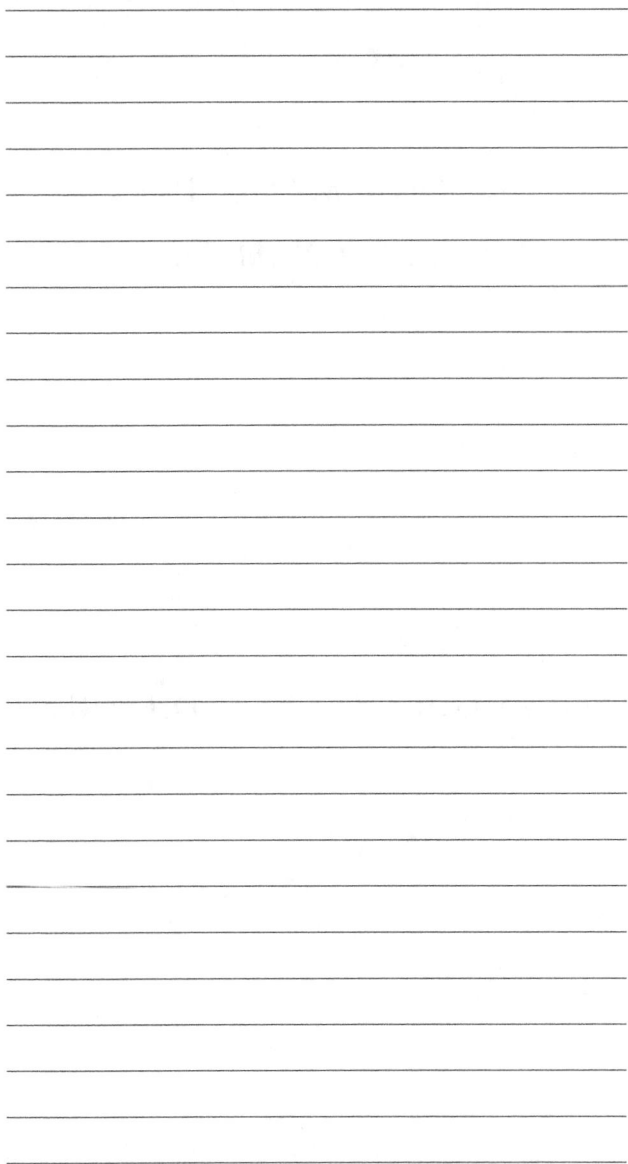

IF ONLY MY MOTHER

HAD TOLD ME...

BOYS & GIRLS ARE VERY DIFFERENT.

#60

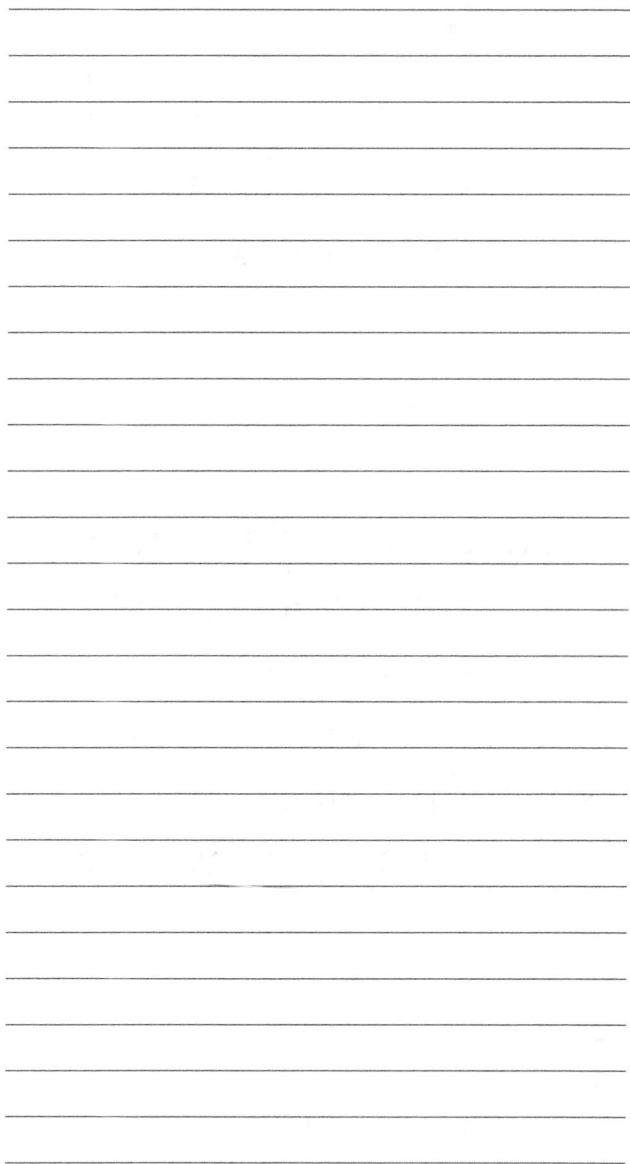

IF ONLY MY MOTHER
HAD TOLD ME...

CHOOSE YOUR LIFE PARTNER
THE WAY YOU CHOOSE
YOUR BEST FRIEND.
IF THEY AREN'T YOUR BEST FRIEND,
YOU MIGHT CHOOSE TO CHOOSE
A DIFFERENT LIFE PARTNER.

#61

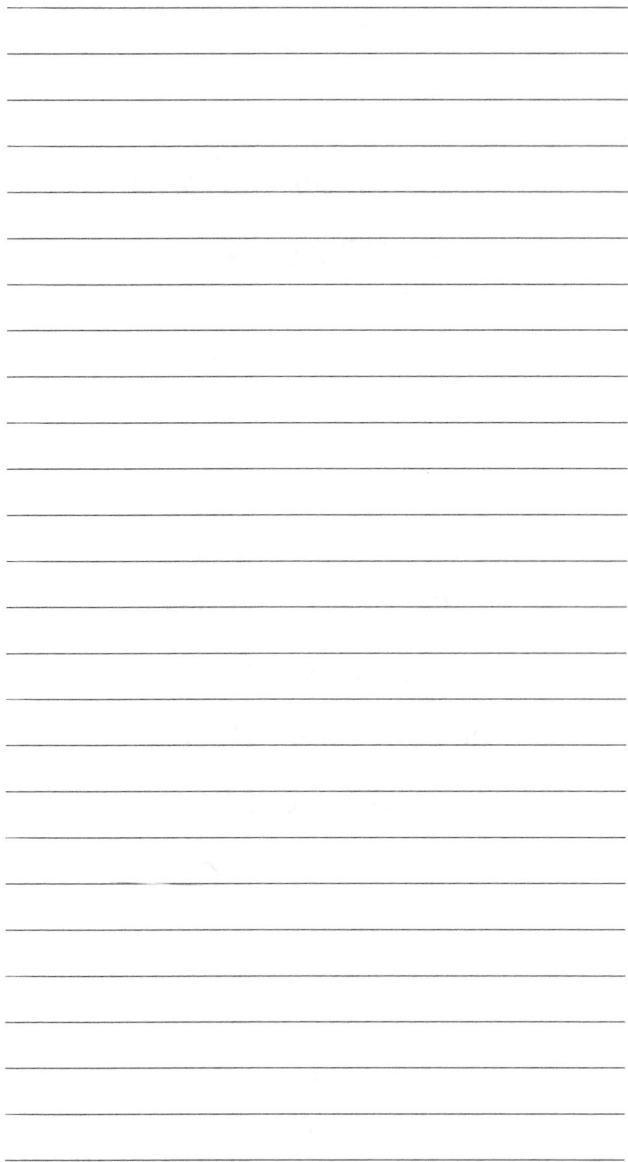

IF ONLY MY MOTHER
HAD TOLD ME...

GOING OUTSIDE
INTO NATURE
ISN'T A PUNISHMENT;
IT'S A GIFT.

#62

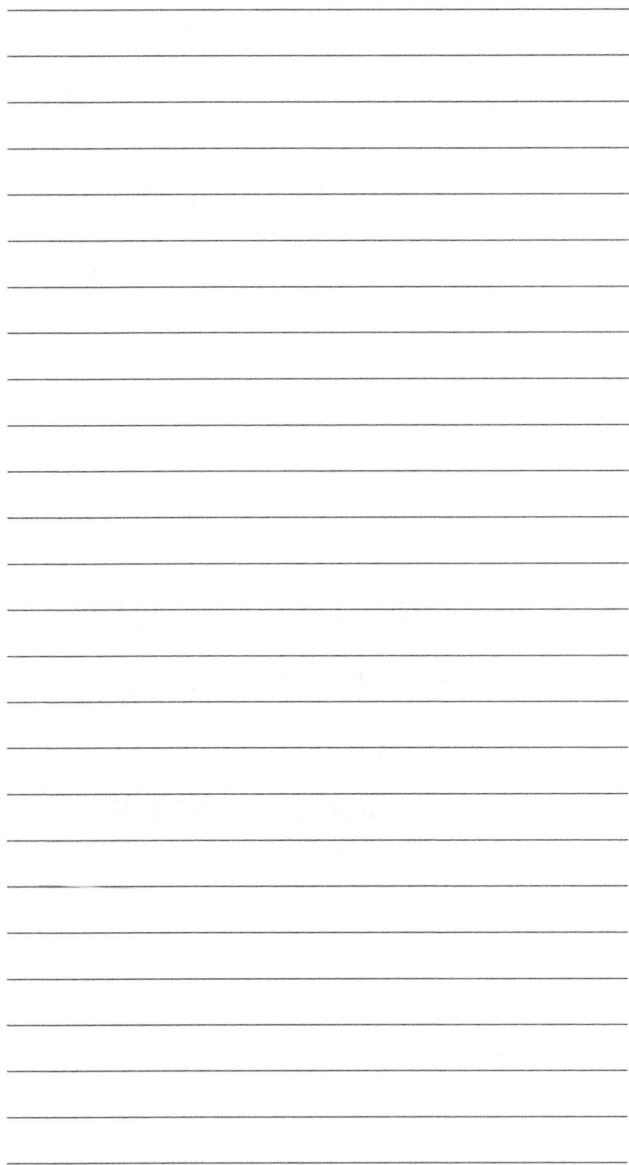

IF ONLY MY MOTHER
HAD TOLD ME...

YOU MIGHT ENJOY SOLITUDE
MORE THAN YOU ENJOY
BEING AROUND PEOPLE.
THIS IS GOOD TO KNOW!

#63

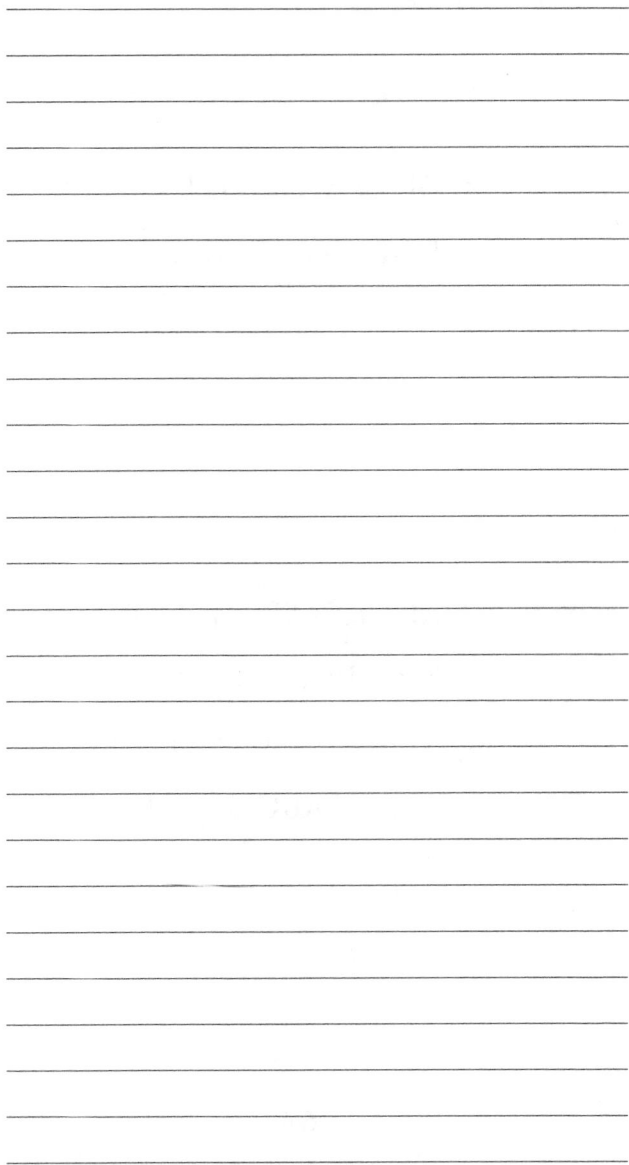

IF ONLY MY MOTHER
HAD TOLD ME...

YOU WERE CREATED TO CREATE.
YOUR NATURAL EXPRESSION
WILL EMERGE ORGANICALLY.
DON'T WORRY ABOUT THE REST.

#64

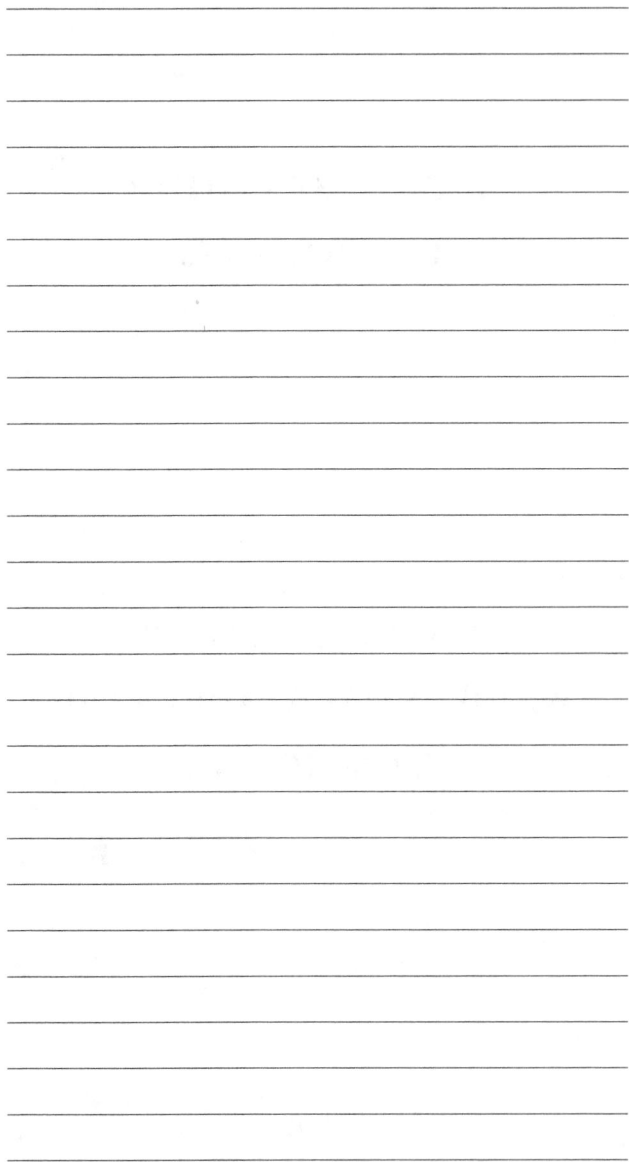

IF ONLY MY MOTHER
HAD TOLD ME...

HEAVEN IS ON EARTH;
WE JUST NEED TO ADJUST OUR
VISION TO SEE IT.

#65

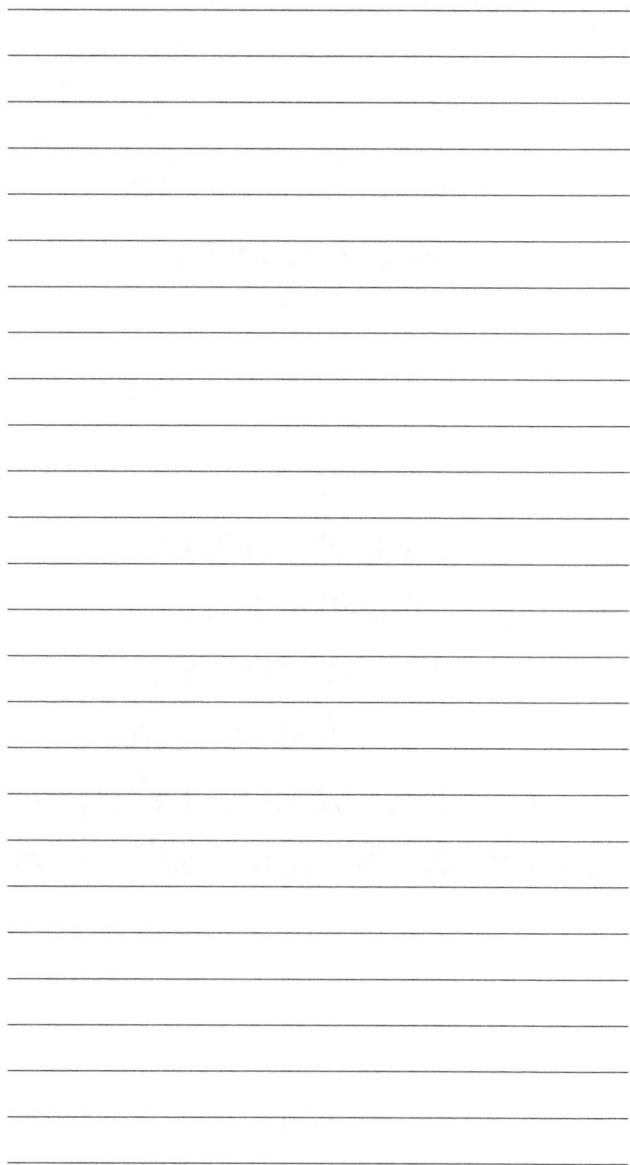

IF ONLY MY MOTHER
HAD TOLD ME...

THERE IS NO UNWORTHY,
NO UNDESERVING,
NO NOT ENOUGH.
I'M TELLING YOU TO
NEVER LET YOURSELF BELIEVE
ANY OF THESE THINGS ABOUT YOU!

#66

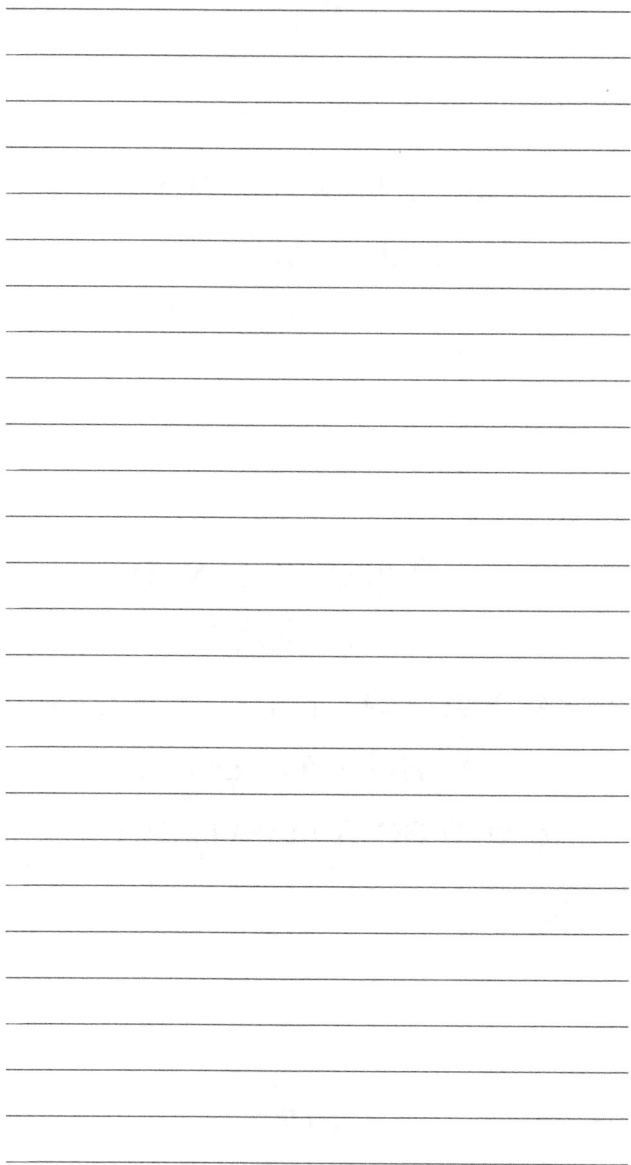

IF ONLY MY MOTHER
HAD TOLD ME...

I AM PROUD OF YOU
FOR BEING YOU.
WHAT YOU DO ISN'T AS IMPORTANT
AS HOW YOU DO IT,
& YOU DO IT MARVELOUSLY!

#67

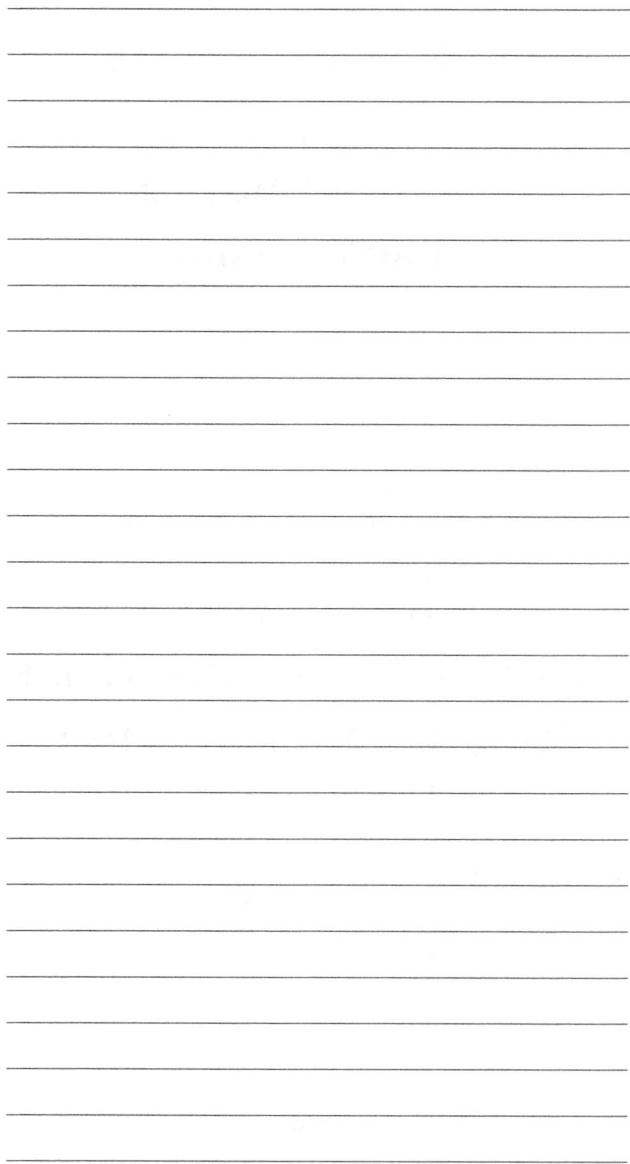

IF ONLY MY MOTHER
HAD TOLD ME...

THERE IS A WAY
TO FORGIVE THE UNFORGIVEABLE.
EVENTUALLY YOU WILL FIND
YOUR WAY.

#68

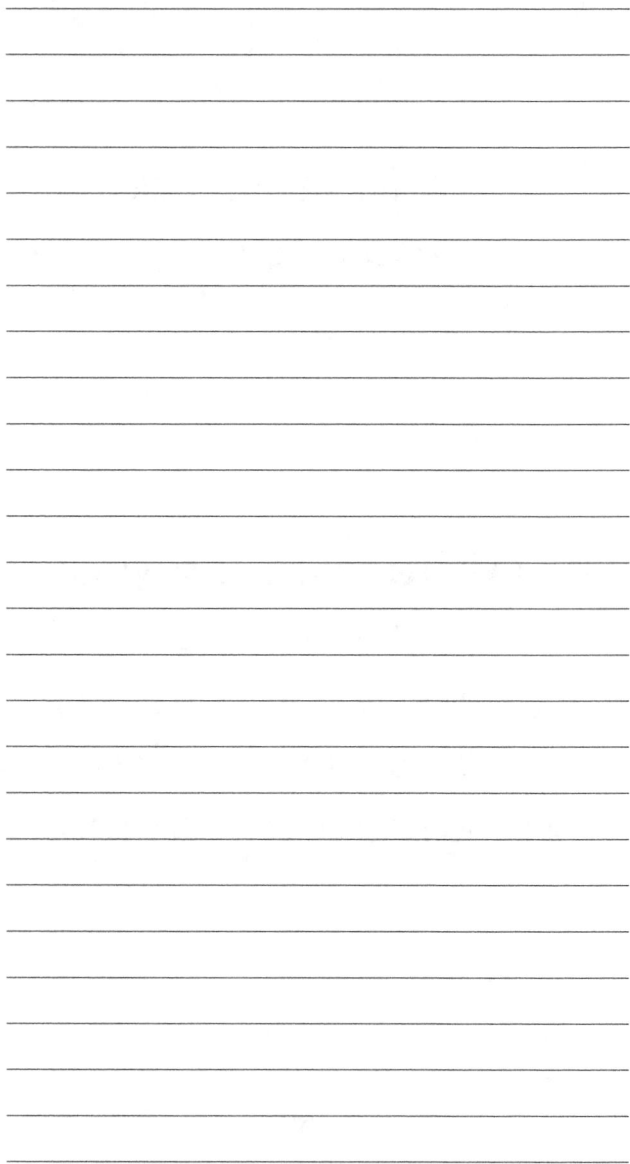

IF ONLY MY MOTHER
HAD TOLD ME...

IT'S EASY TO LOVE THE LOVEABLE.
WHAT ABOUT THOSE
WHO ACT IN WAYS
THAT AREN'T SO LOVEABLE?
WE HAVE TO LOVE THEM TOO!

#69

IF ONLY MY MOTHER
HAD TOLD ME...

.

IF YOU ARE GIVING TO GET,
YOU'LL MISS OUT ON THE FUN
OF GIVING TO GIVE.

#70

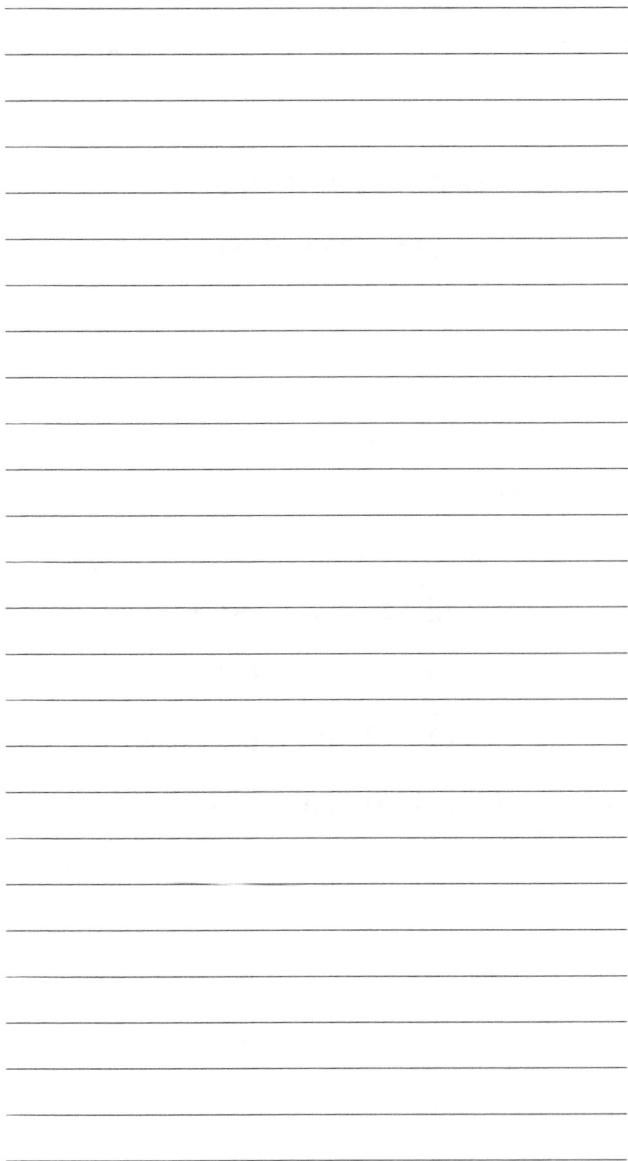

IF ONLY MY MOTHER
HAD TOLD ME...

CLEAN YOUR ROOM,
ONLY BECAUSE
YOU'LL FEEL BETTER
FOR HAVING DONE SO.

#71

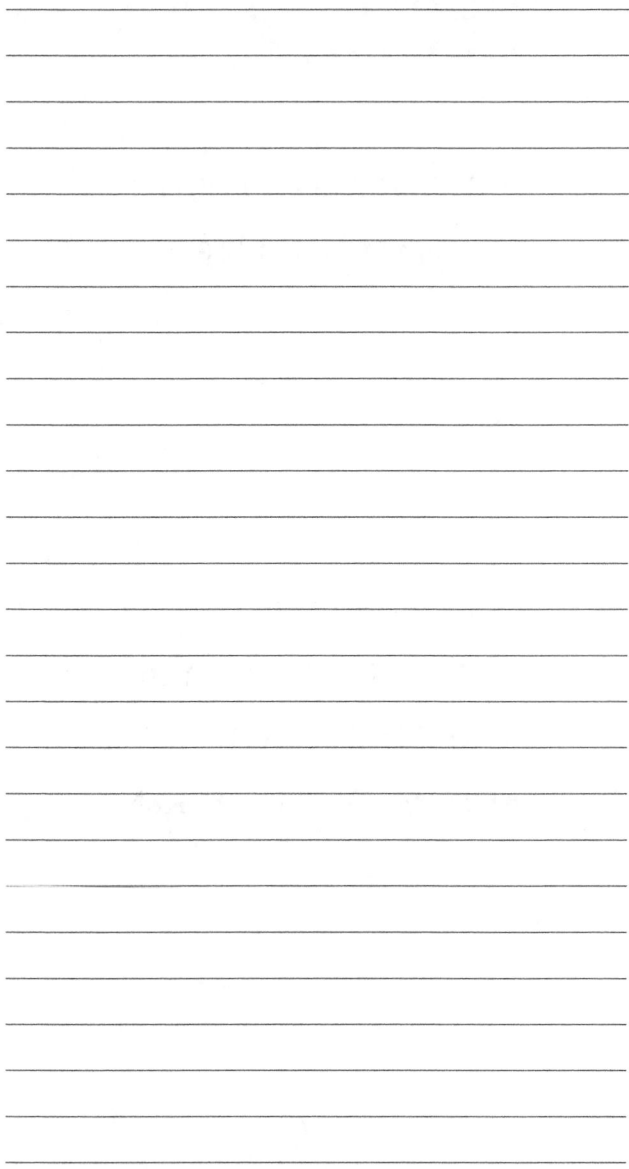

IF ONLY MY MOTHER
HAD TOLD ME...

BE YOU.
AND I CAN LOVE YOU
MORE THAN IF YOU TRY TO
BE SOMEONE DIFFERENT.

#72

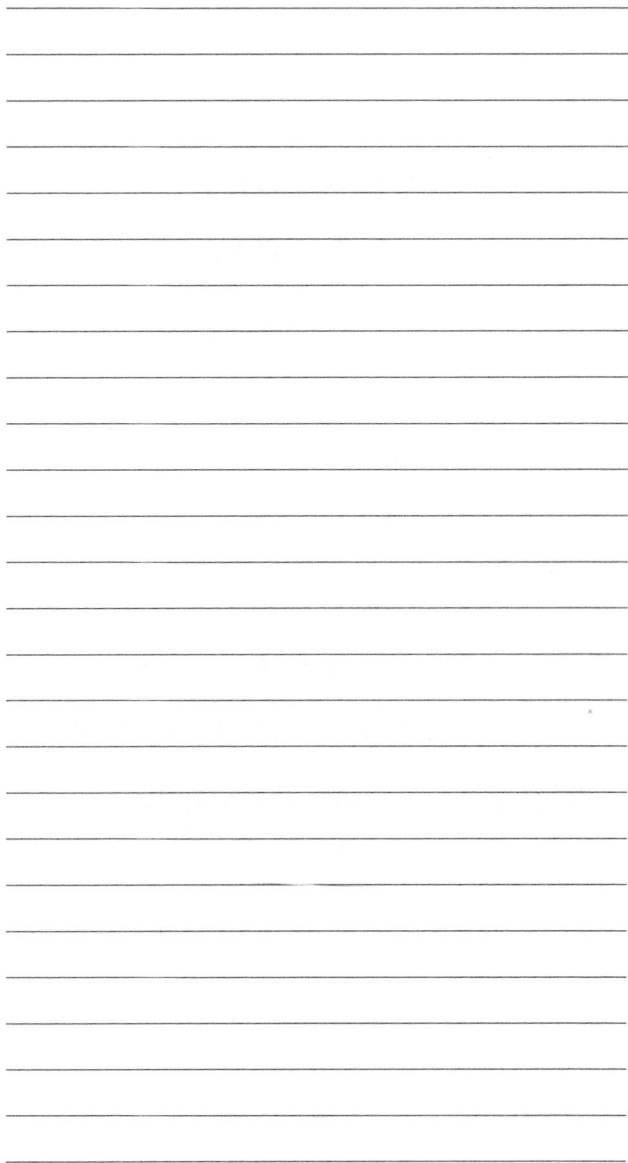

IF ONLY MY MOTHER
HAD TOLD ME...

IT TAKES COURAGE
TO LIVE YOUR OWN LIFE,
ESPECIALLY WHEN IT MEANS
REJECTING CONSENSUS REALITY.

#73

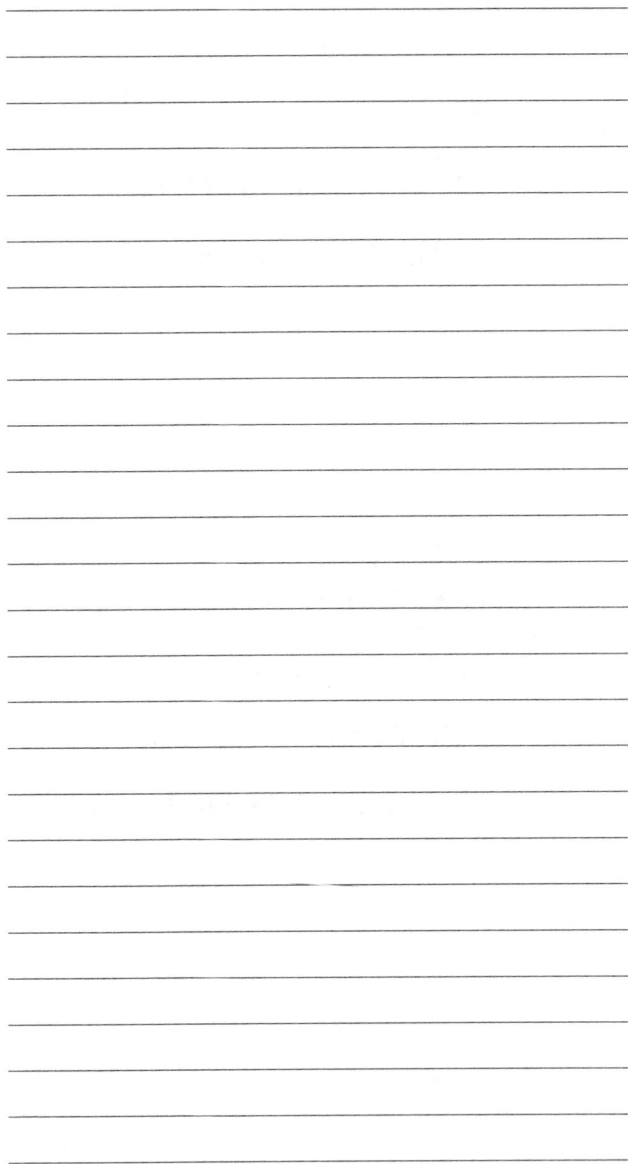

IF ONLY MY MOTHER
HAD TOLD ME...

YOU ARE ALREADY WHOLE.
IT'S JUST A MATTER
OF REMEMBERING
THAT THIS IS TRUE.

#74

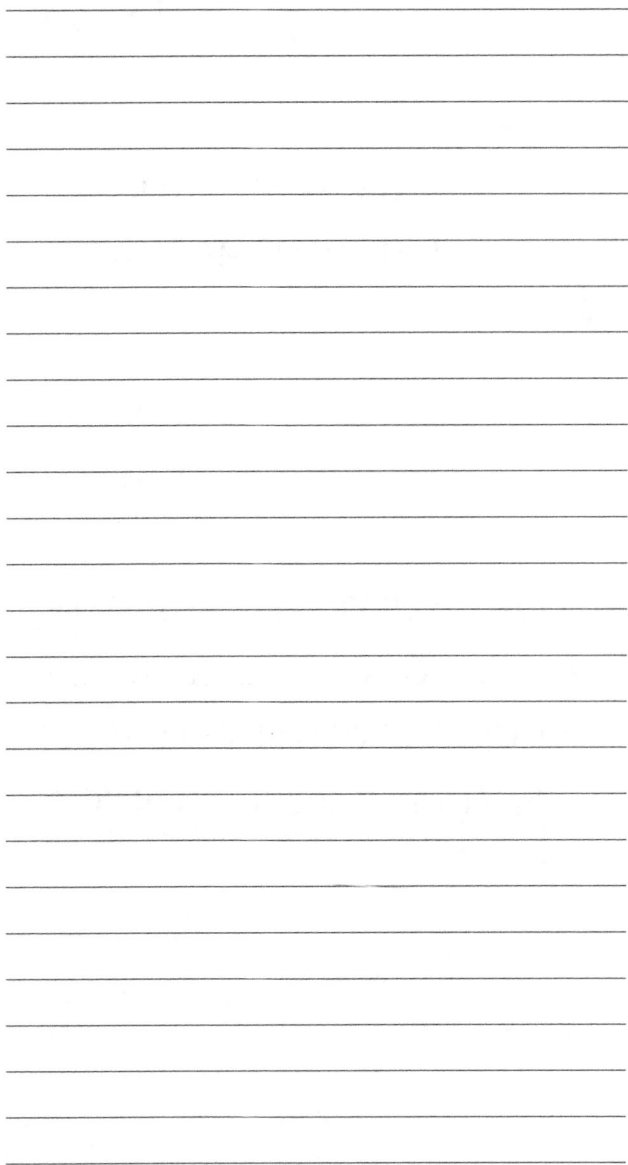

IF ONLY MY MOTHER
HAD TOLD ME...

OUR FAVORITE PEOPLE IN LIFE
ARE THE ONE'S THAT SOMEHOW
LET US KNOW THAT THEY SEE US,
BEHIND OUR PRETENDING.

#75

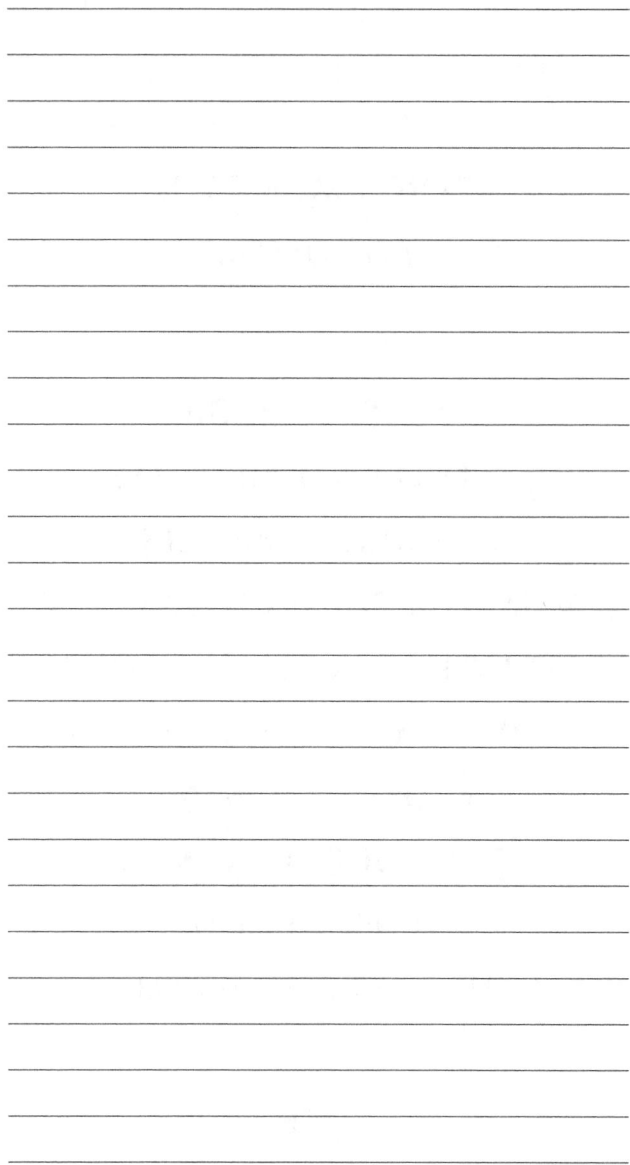

IF ONLY MY MOTHER
HAD TOLD ME...

THERE IS MAGIC,
& THERE ARE MIRACLES,
& FAIRIES & ANGELS,
& UNSEEN GUIDES TO ASSIST US
AT EVERY TURN IN THE ROAD.
SOMETIMES THEY ARE QUIET,
BECAUSE THEY WANT US
TO USE OUR OWN SMARTS
TO FIGURE OUT
THE NEXT STEP TO TAKE.

#76

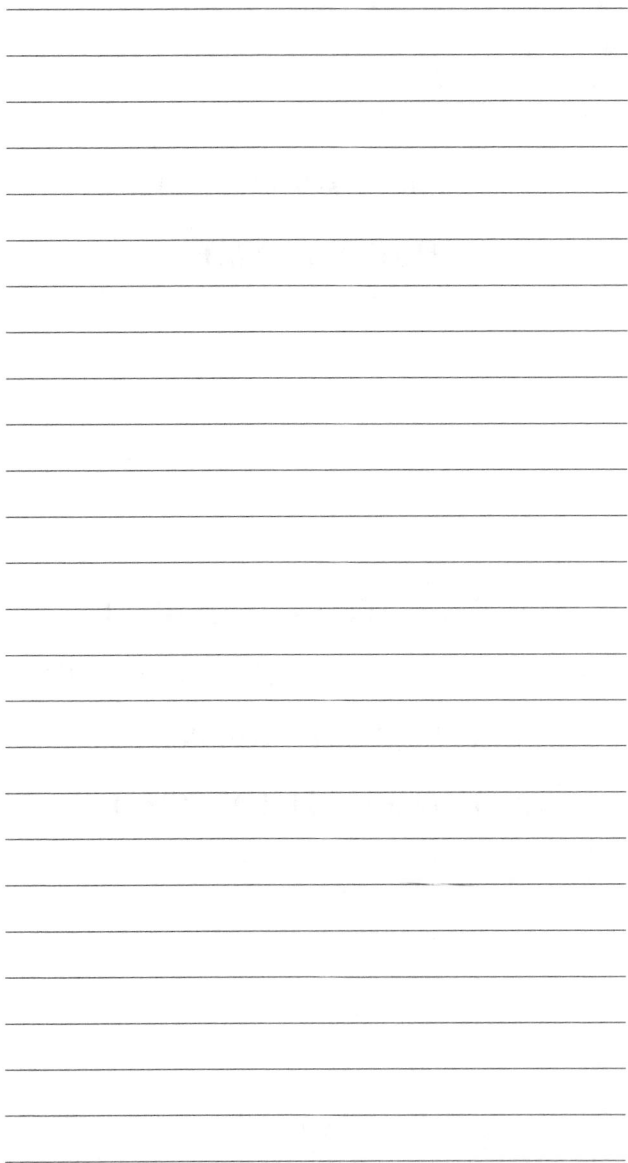

IF ONLY MY MOTHER
HAD TOLD ME...

HAVING FAITH IN YOURSELF &
IN WHAT YOU BELIEVE TO BE TRUE
IS THE MOST IMPORTANT
THING IN THE WORLD.

#77

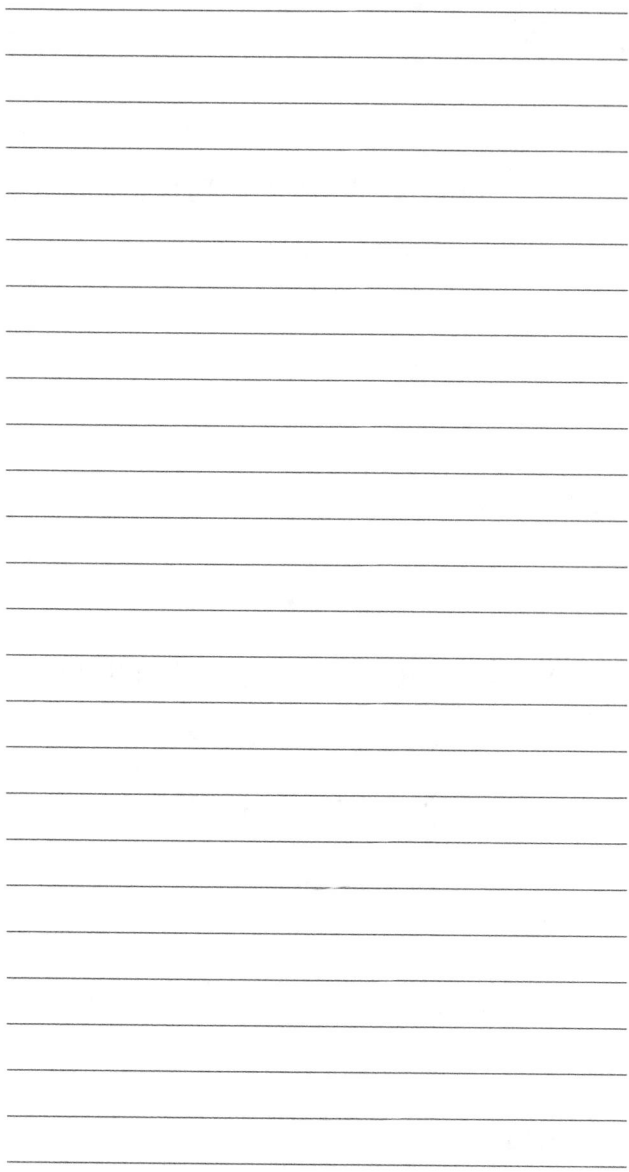

IF ONLY MY MOTHER
HAD TOLD ME...

GOD IS
WHAT YOU MAKE HIM/HER/IT:
NOTHING MORE;
NOTHING LESS.

#78

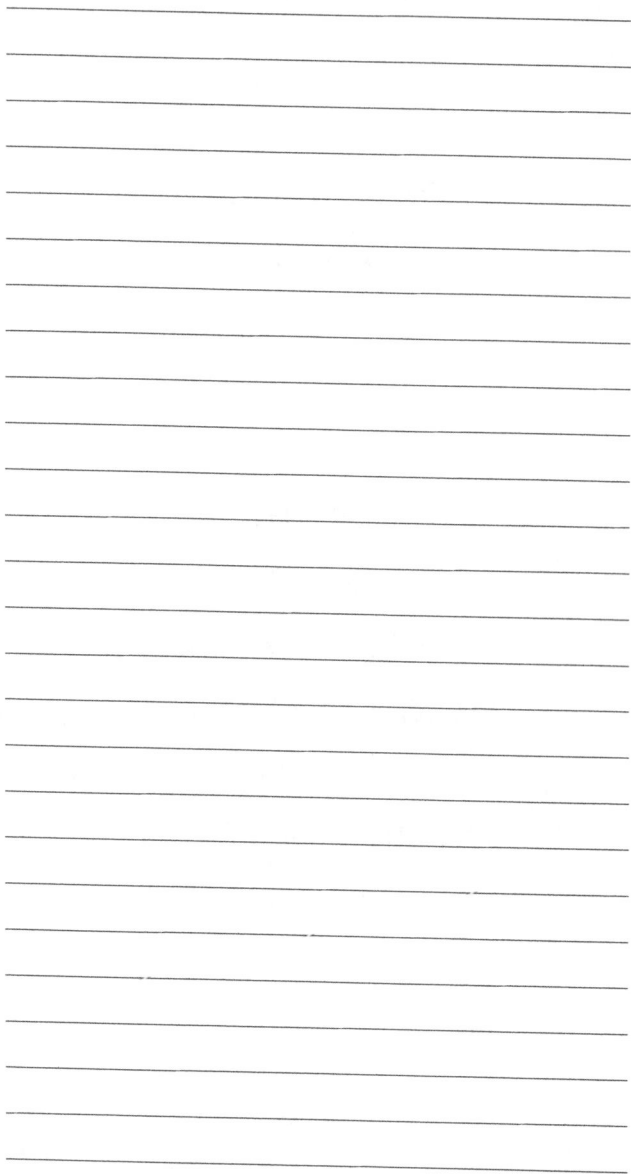

IF ONLY MY MOTHER
HAD TOLD ME...

OVERWHELM
IS JUST TRYING
TO DO TOO MUCH
ALL AT THE SAME TIME.
SLOW DOWN.
TAKE JUST ONE THING
AT A TIME.

#79

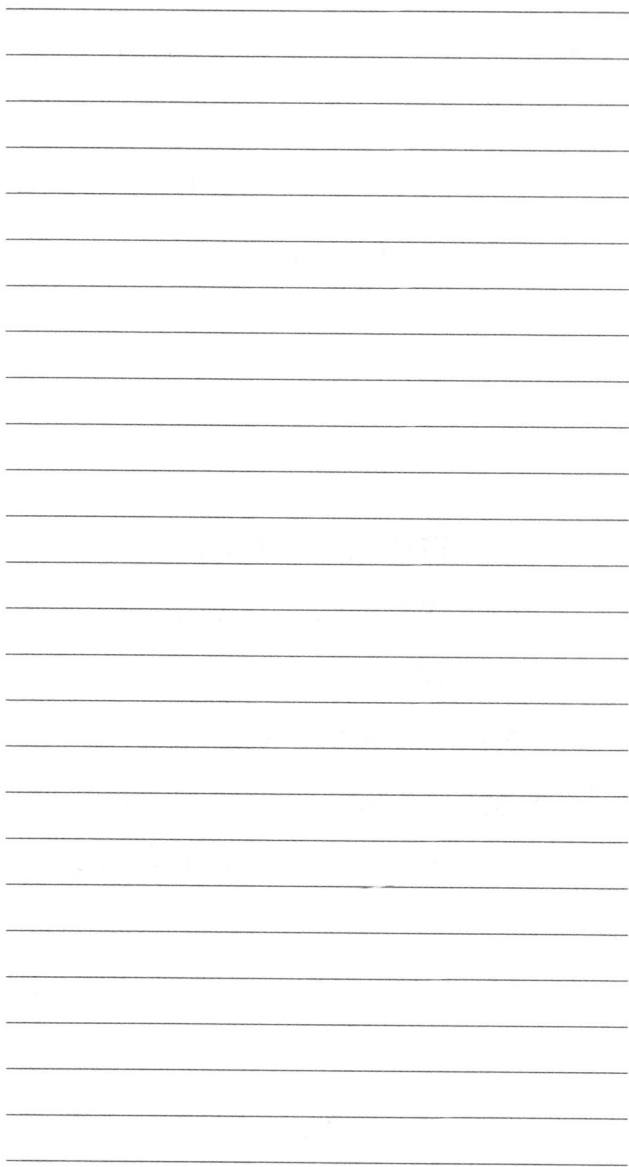

IF ONLY MY MOTHER
HAD TOLD ME...

THERE IS ALWAYS
MORE THAN ENOUGH
TO GO AROUND.
YOU CAN HAVE ALL THE FUN
YOU ARE WILLING TO HAVE
& SO CAN EVERYONE ELSE.

#80

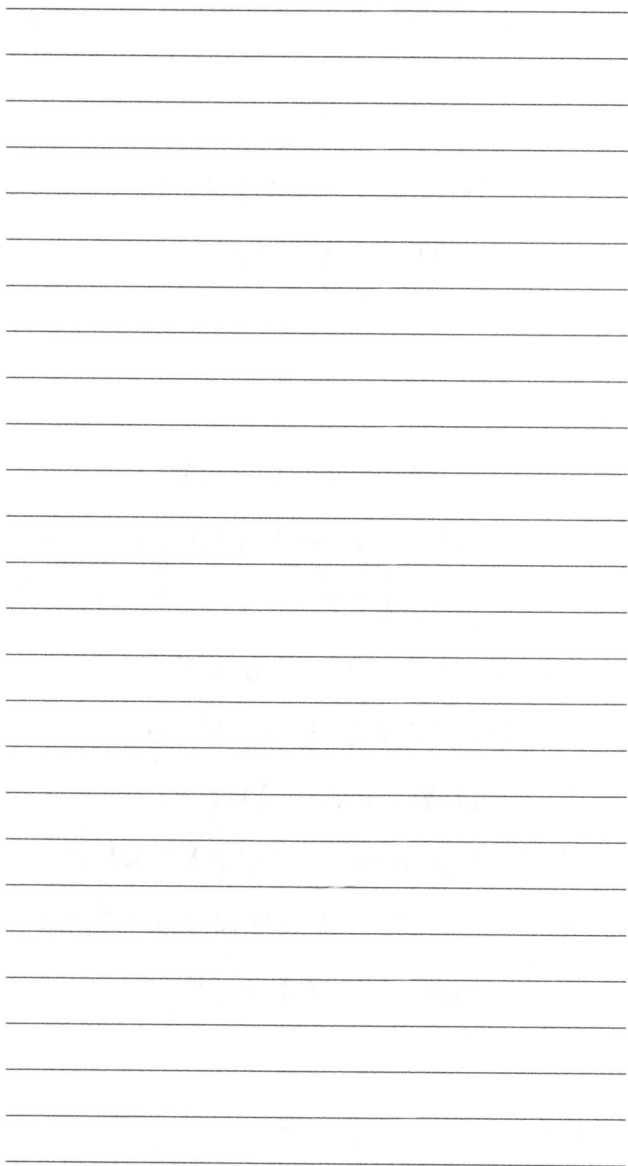

IF ONLY MY MOTHER
HAD TOLD ME...

AT SOME POINT,
YOUR BODY WILL SAG &
YOU WON'T RECOGNIZE THE
PERSON STARING BACK AT YOU
THROUGH THE MIRROR.
AND, YOU MAY FIND THAT
YOU LOVE YOURSELF MORE IN
THIS MOMENT THAN YOU EVER
THOUGHT POSSIBLE.

#81

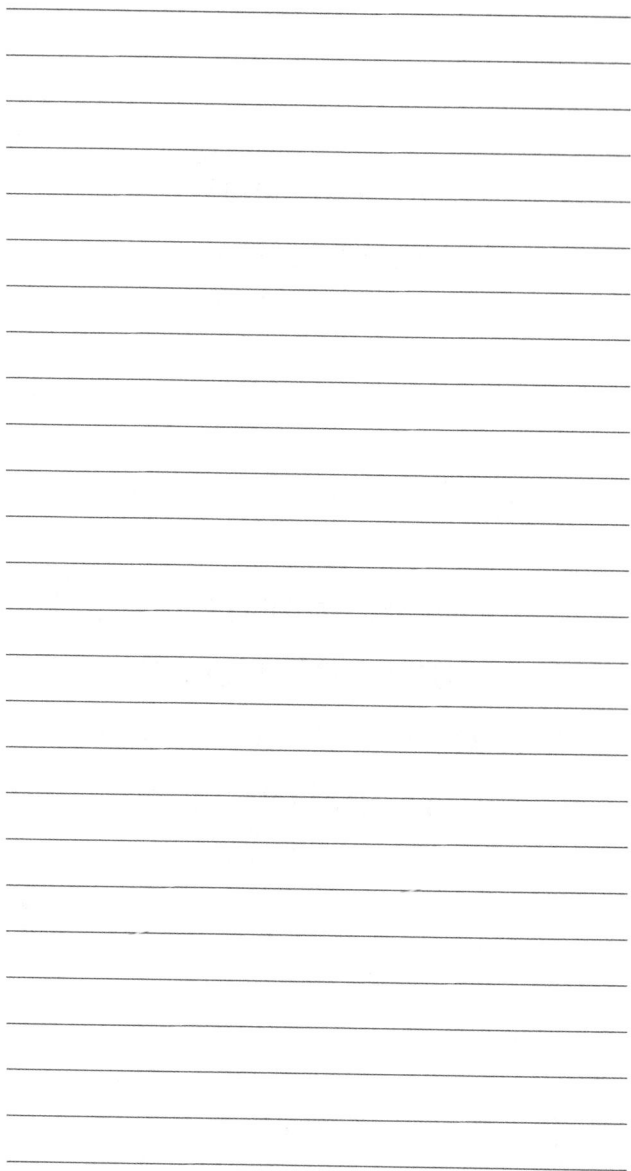

IF ONLY MY MOTHER
HAD TOLD ME...

YOU CAN'T CREATE PEACE
OUT IN THE WORLD.
YOU CAN ONLY CREATE PEACE
WITHIN YOURSELF.

#82

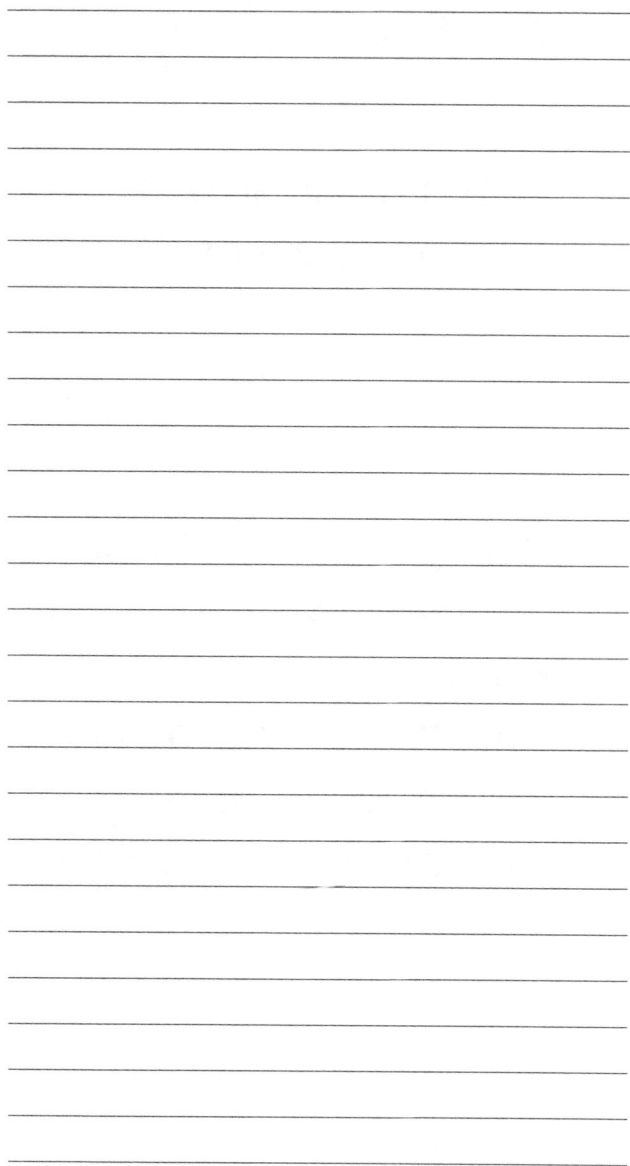

IF ONLY MY MOTHER
HAD TOLD ME...

YOU NEVER STOP GROWING,
YOU NEVER STOP LEARNING,
& AS LONG AS YOU ARE BREATHING
YOU NEVER STOP CULTIVATING
OPPORTUNITIES
TO LOVE YOURSELF BETTER.

#83

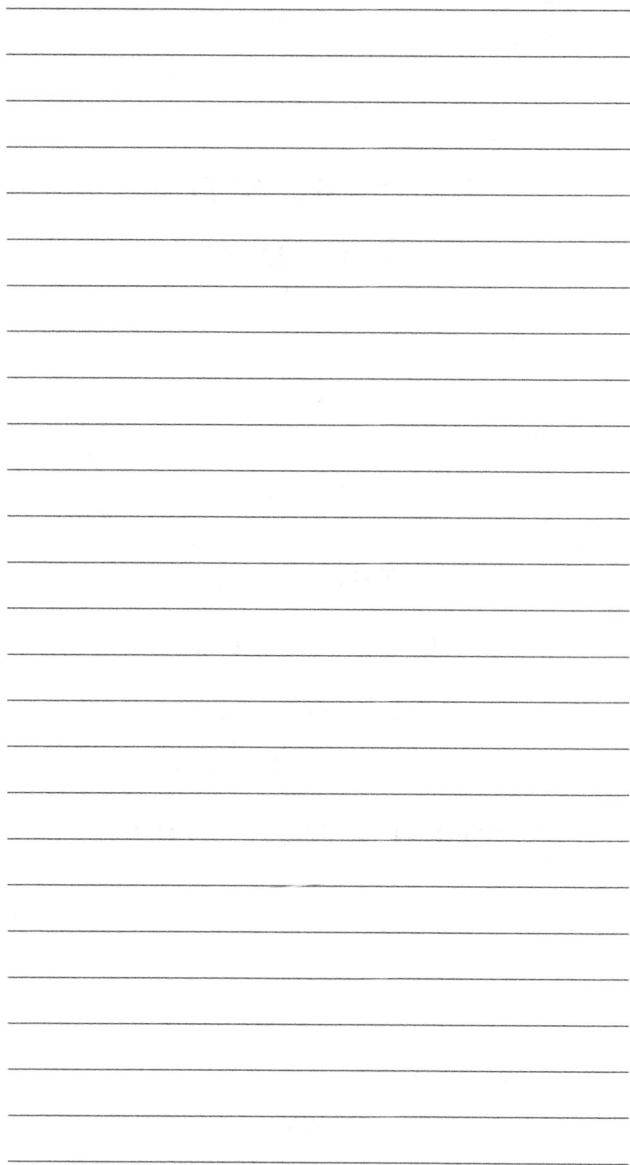

IF ONLY MY MOTHER
HAD TOLD ME...

THE MORE
YOU GENERATE LOVE
INSIDE YOUR SELF,
THE MORE LOVE
THERE IS IN THE WORLD.

#84

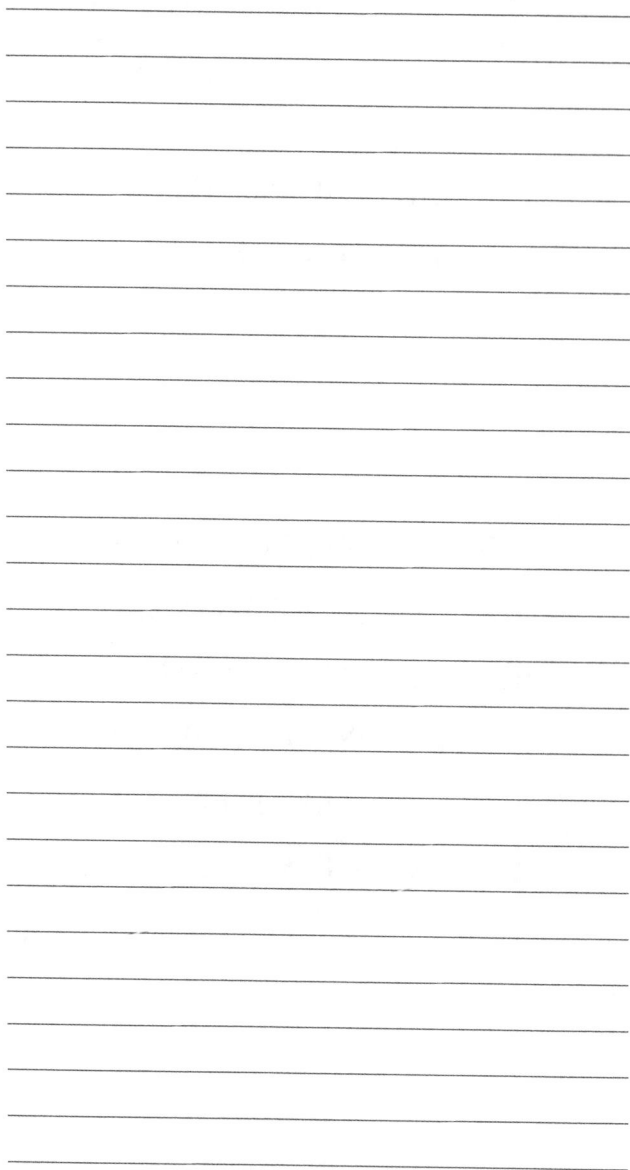

IF ONLY MY MOTHER
HAD TOLD ME...

SOMETIMES YOUR LIFE
WILL REQUIRE PHYSICAL
DISCOMFORT & EMOTIONAL
AGONY IN ORDER
TO HEAL ITSELF.
IT SUCKS, & IT'S NECESSARY.

#85

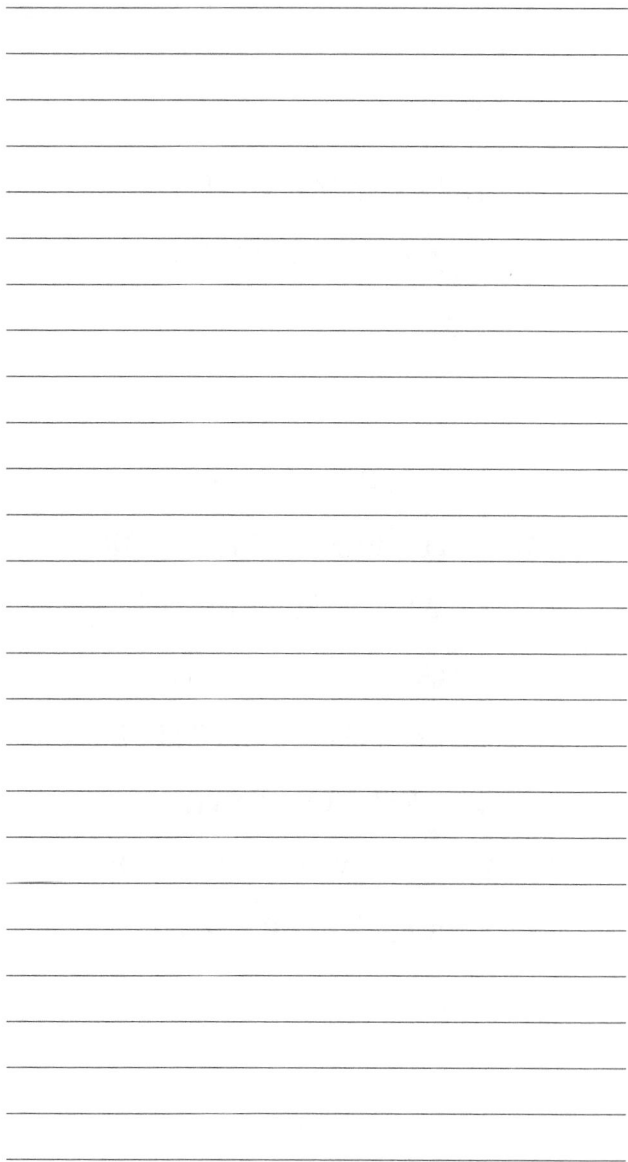

IF ONLY MY MOTHER
HAD TOLD ME...

THERE ARE A LOT
OF MOTHERS IN THE WORLD
THAT SEE YOU BETTER
THAN I CAN SEE YOU.
FIND THE ONES THAT
SEE YOU BEST.
I WILL ALWAYS LOVE YOU,
NO MATTER WHAT.

#86

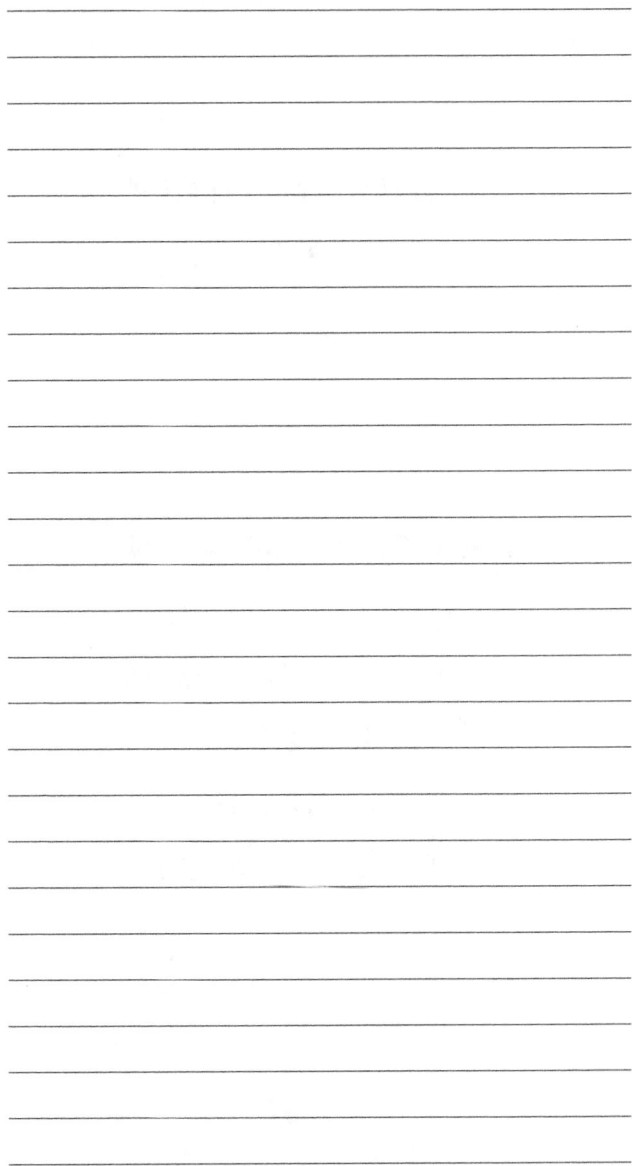

IF ONLY MY MOTHER
HAD TOLD ME...

YOUR CHILDREN WON'T
ALWAYS LIKE YOU,
& YOU WON'T ALWAYS
LIKE THEM,
BUT THE LOVE
NEVER GOES AWAY.

#87

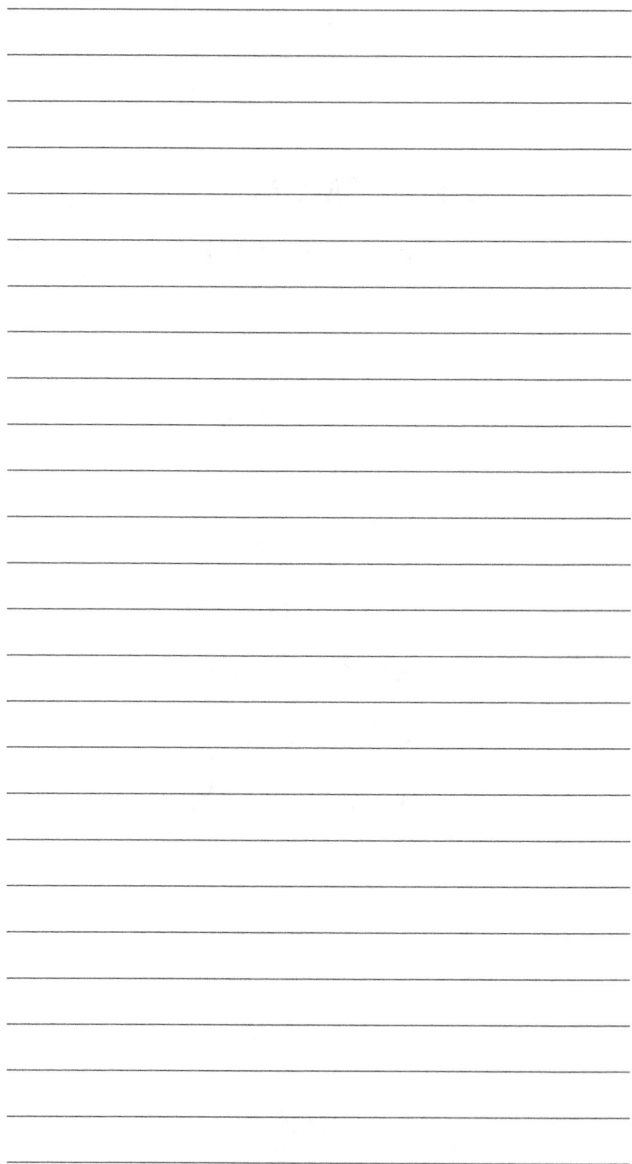

IF ONLY MY MOTHER

HAD TOLD ME...

ASK THE TOUGH

QUESTIONS

& SAY WHAT'S

HARD TO SAY.

#88

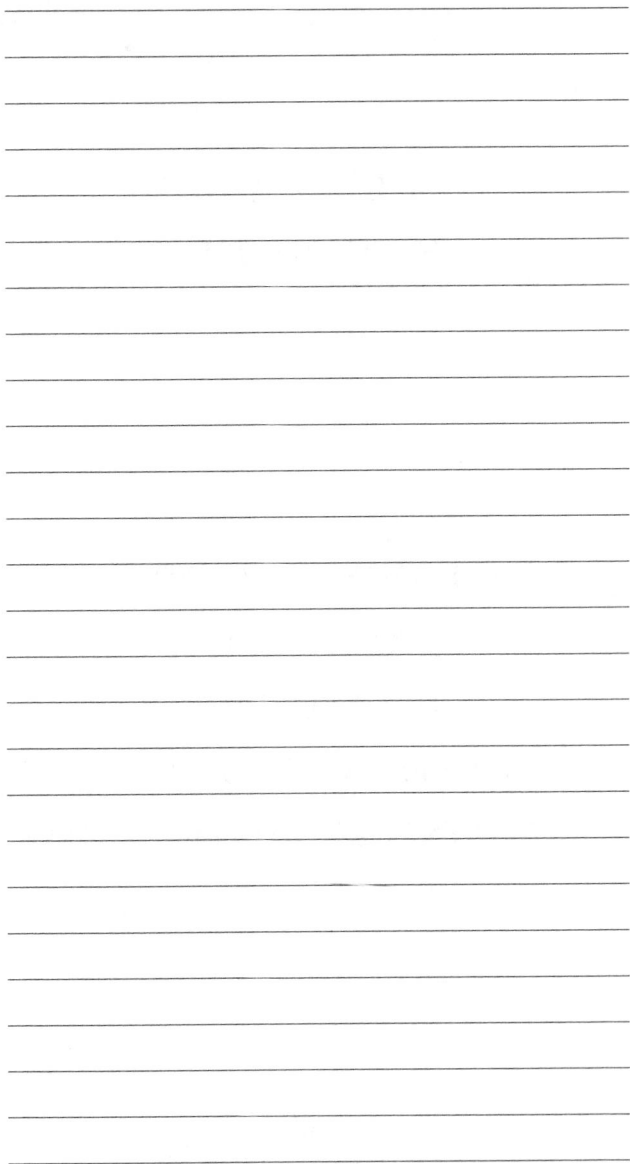

IF ONLY MY MOTHER
HAD TOLD ME...

LIFE IS ONE, LONG, ONGOING
CONVERSATION.
JUST KEEP TALKING;
AND, BEING A GOOD LISTENER
MAKES IT ALL THE MORE FUN.

#89

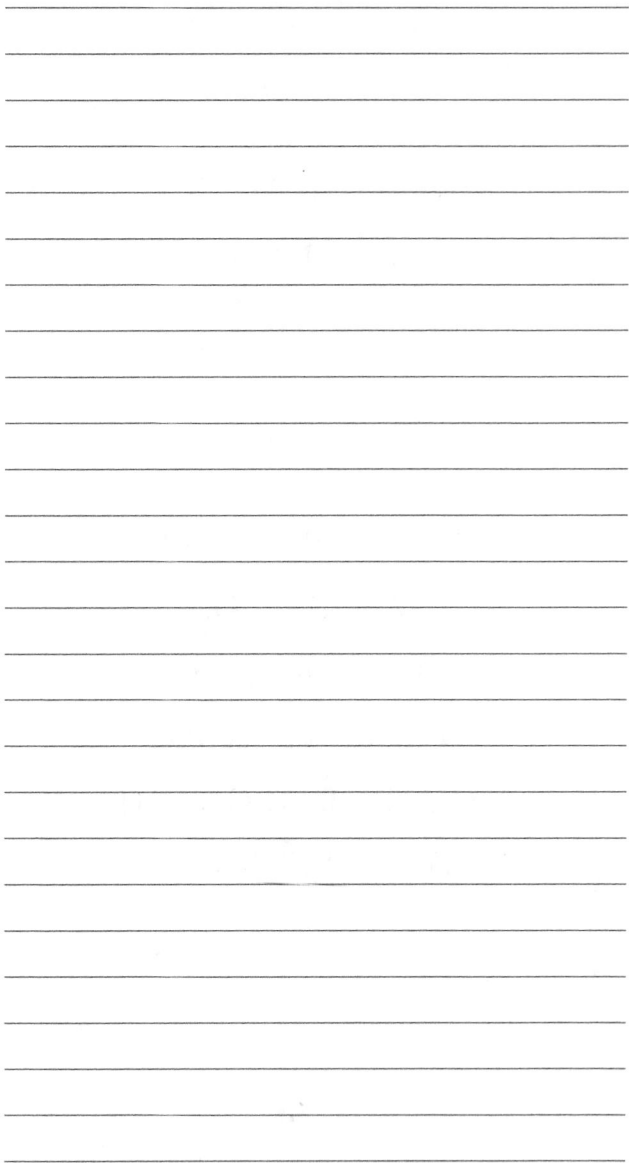

IF ONLY MY MOTHER
HAD TOLD ME...

YOU CAN'T KNOW
ABOUT LIFE
FROM A BOOK
OR FROM SCHOOL.
YOU HAVE TO GO OUT
& EXPERIENCE IT.

#90

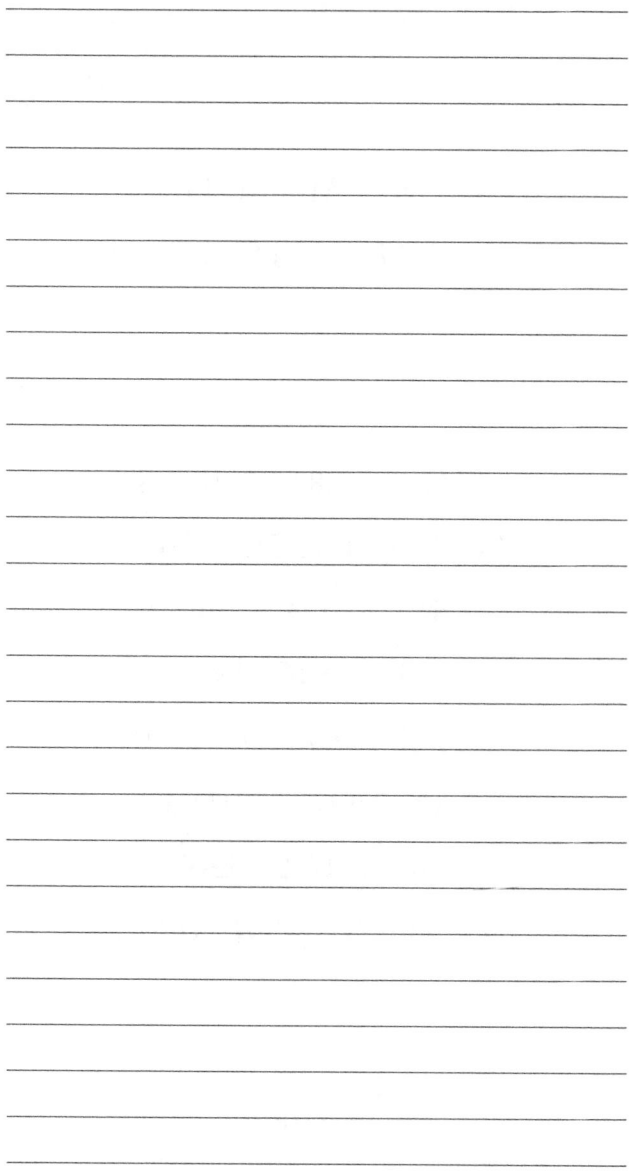

IF ONLY MY MOTHER
HAD TOLD ME...

THERE ARE THINGS
YOU WILL HAVE TO DO,
LIKE GO TO SCHOOL,
& PLAY NICE WITH
PEOPLE YOU DON'T LIKE.
FIND THE THINGS
THAT ARE LIKEABLE
AMONG THE UNLIKEABLE.

#91

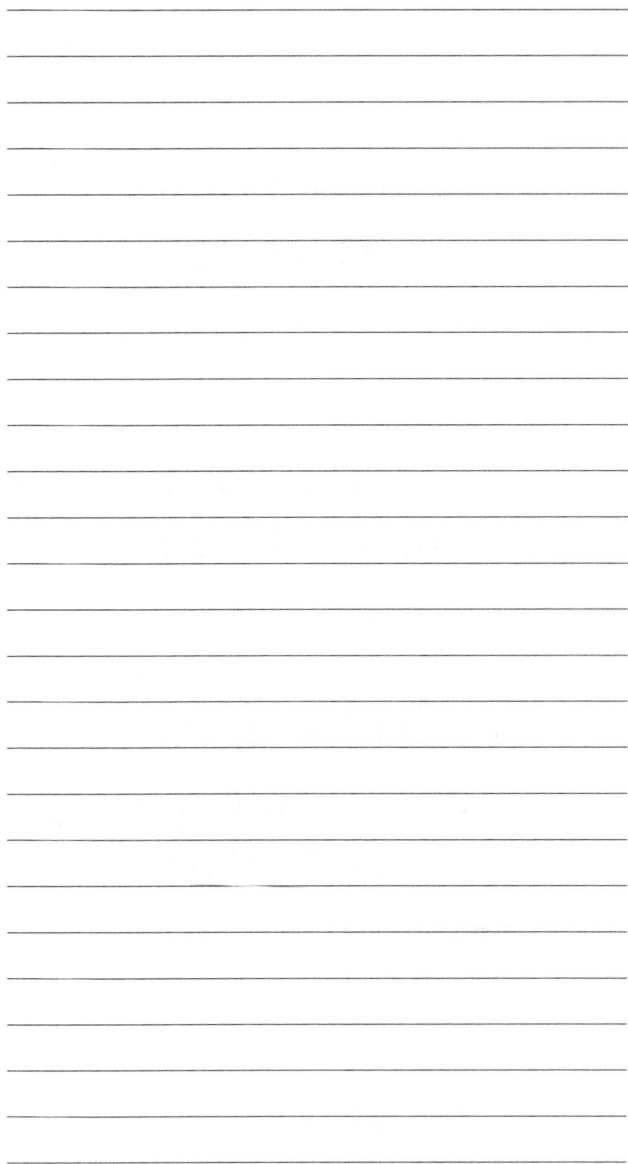

IF ONLY MY MOTHER
HAD TOLD ME...

MONEY DOESN'T
COME FROM PEOPLE,
FROM WORK,
OR FROM WHAT YOU DO.
THE UNIVERSE IS THE
SOURCE OF ALL OF IT.
YOUR JOB IS TO
BE OPEN TO RECEIVING.

#92

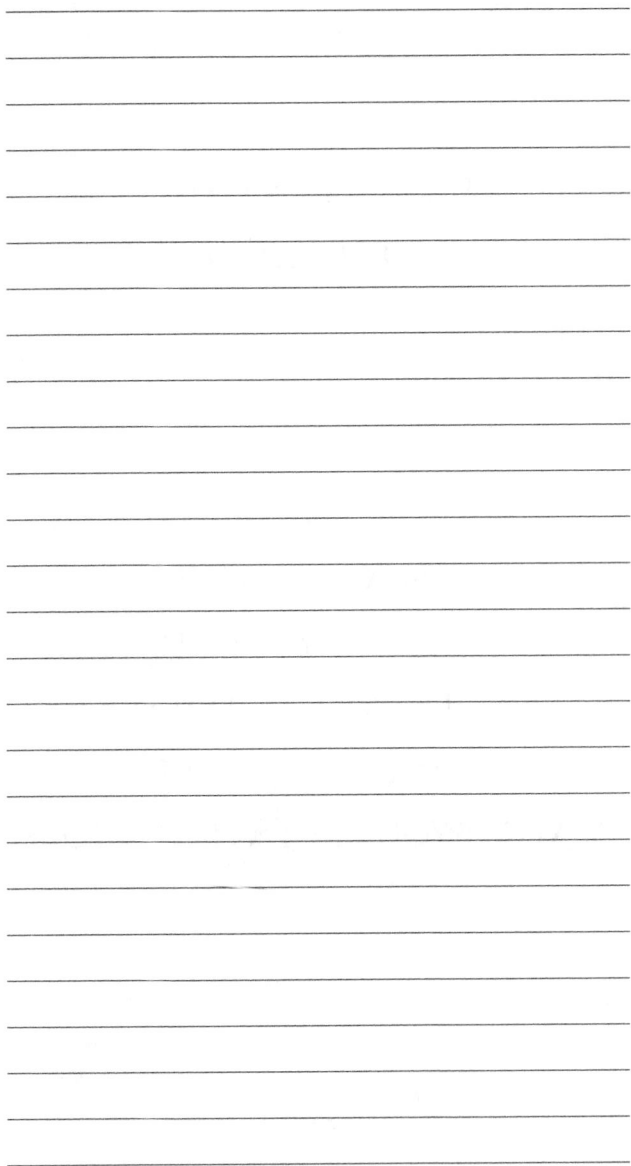

IF ONLY MY MOTHER
HAD TOLD ME...

YOU CAN BELIEVE
YOU'RE ENTITLED,
BUT THAT DOESN'T
MEAN YOU'LL GET
WHAT YOU ARE ENTITLED TO.

#93

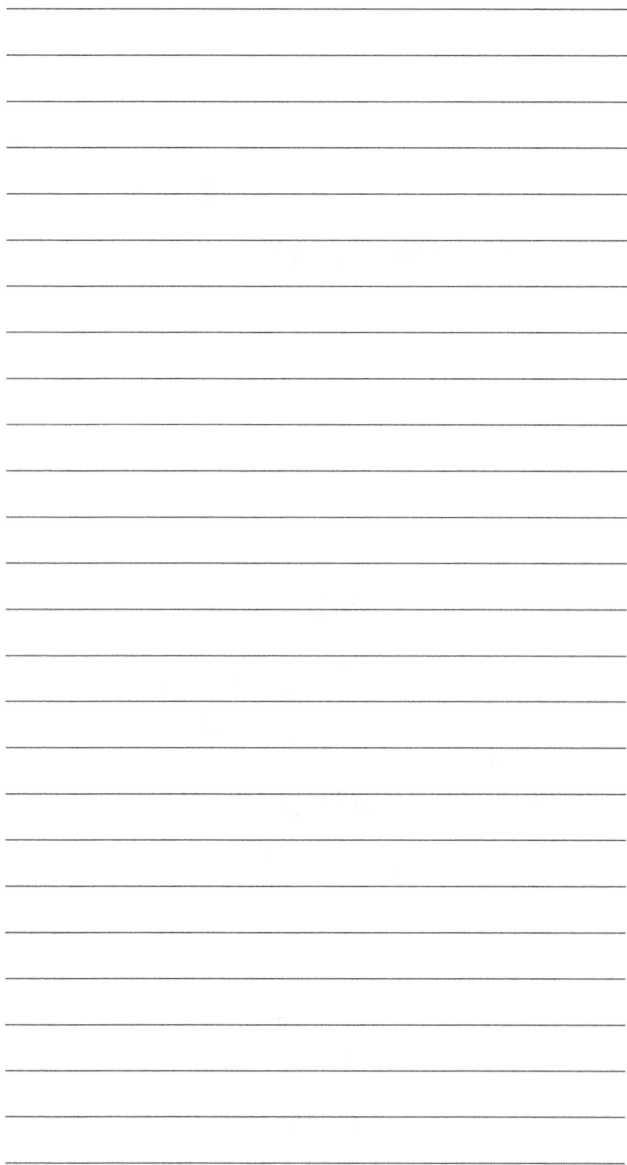

IF ONLY MY MOTHER
HAD TOLD ME...

SOMETIMES
THERE'S NOTHING
YOU CAN DO
BUT CRY.

#94

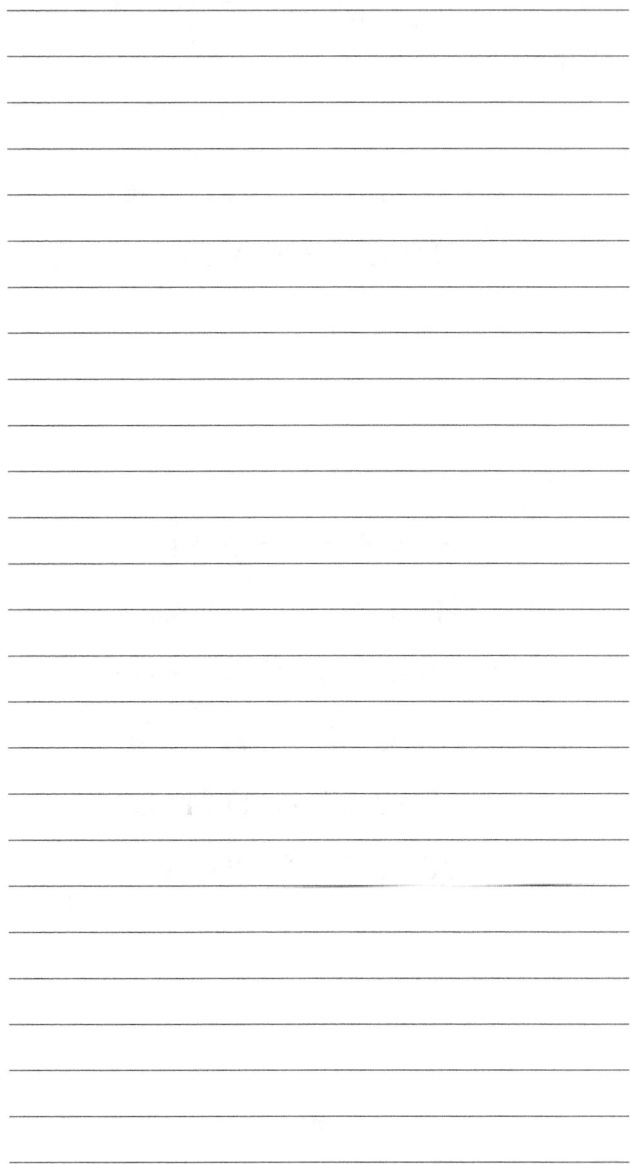

IF ONLY MY MOTHER
HAD TOLD ME...

SOMETIMES JUST
THE TINIEST THING
WILL MAKE YOU SO HAPPY
TO BE ALIVE–
EVEN A TINY, LITTLE,
FURRY CATERPILLAR.

#95

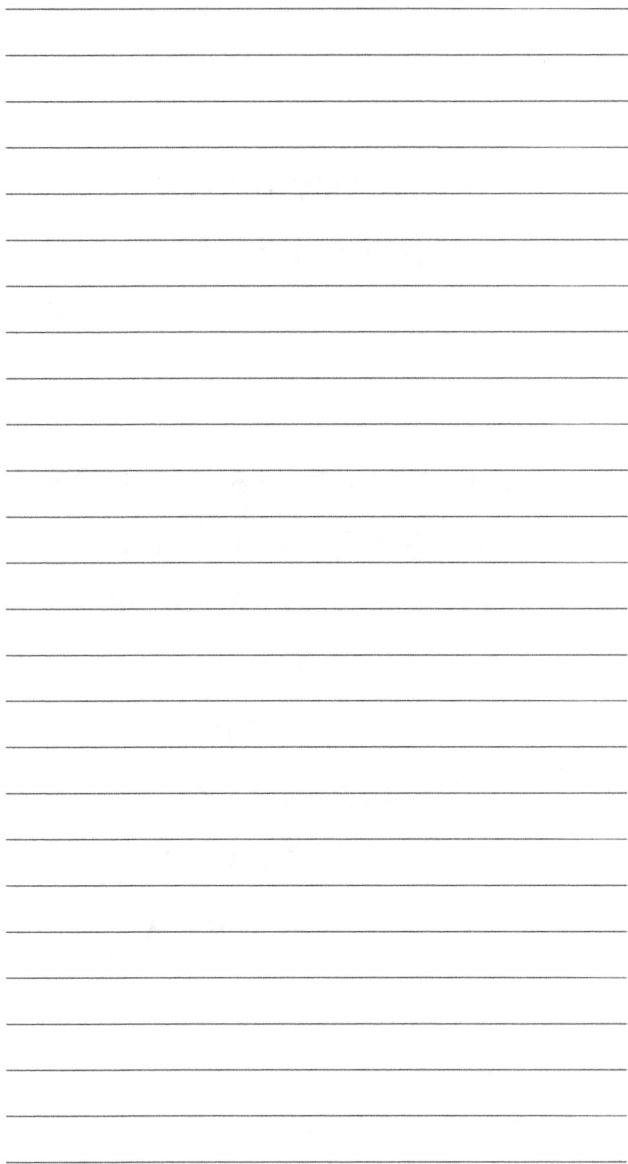

IF ONLY MY MOTHER
HAD TOLD ME...

MOMS & DADS TEACH A LOT,
EVEN WHEN THEY'RE
NOT SAYING ANYTHING.
CHILDREN WILL
LEARN FROM
WHAT THEY SEE,
NOT NECESSARILY
FROM WHAT YOU SAY.

#96

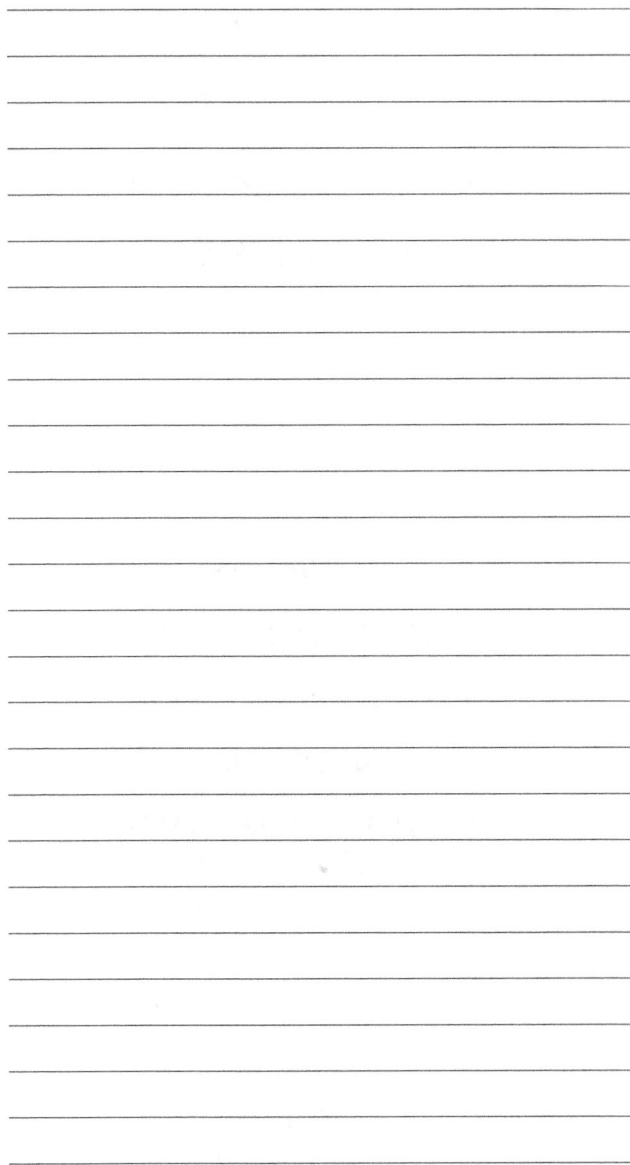

IF ONLY MY MOTHER
HAD TOLD ME...

SOMETIMES,
YOUR CHILDREN
HAVE TO REJECT YOU
IN ORDER
TO FIND THEMSELVES.

#97

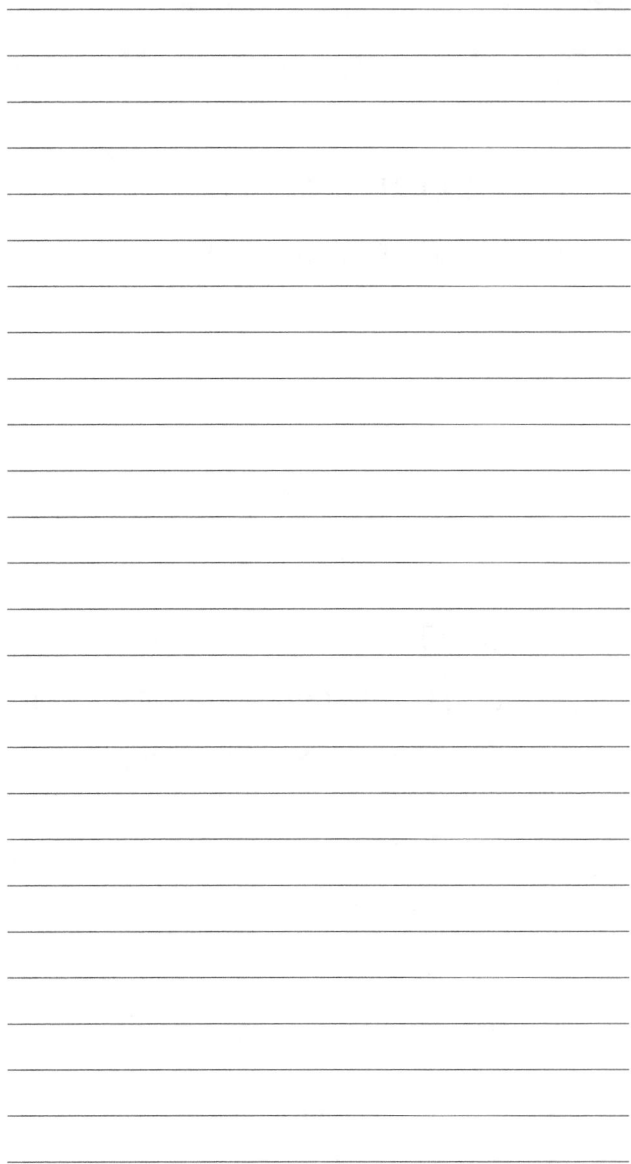

IF ONLY MY MOTHER
HAD TOLD ME...

MAKE IT AS EASY AS POSSIBLE
FOR OTHER PEOPLE TO BE GLAD
THEY ARE WHO THEY ARE.

#98

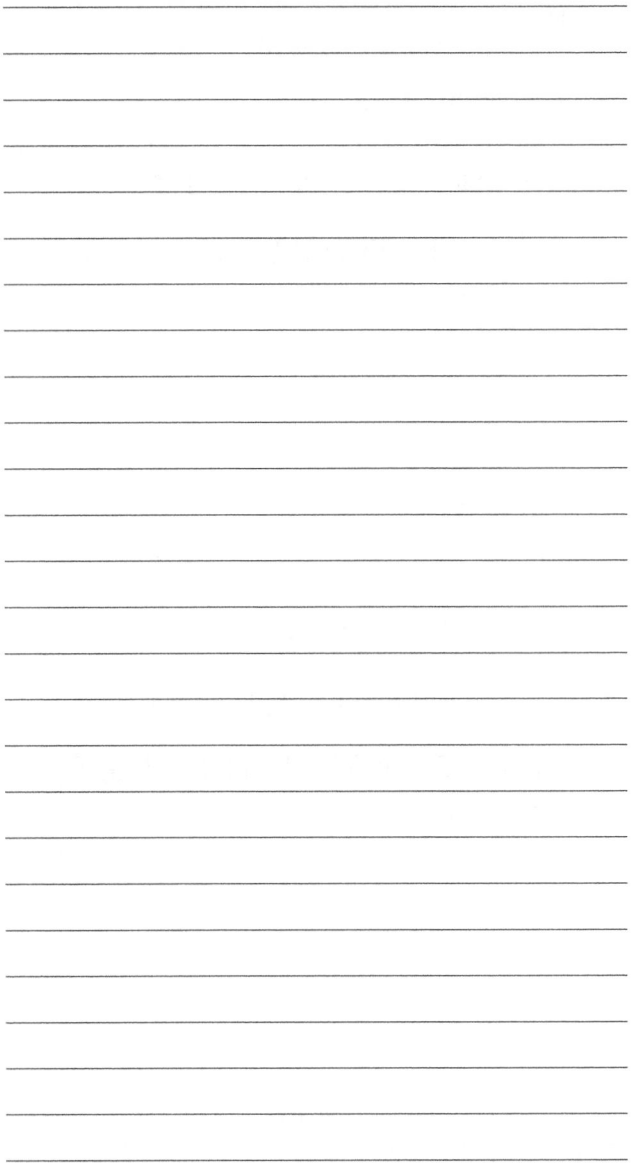

IF ONLY MY MOTHER
HAD TOLD ME...

BE GENEROUS
WITH YOUR HEART.
THERE'S NOTHING TO LOSE.

#99

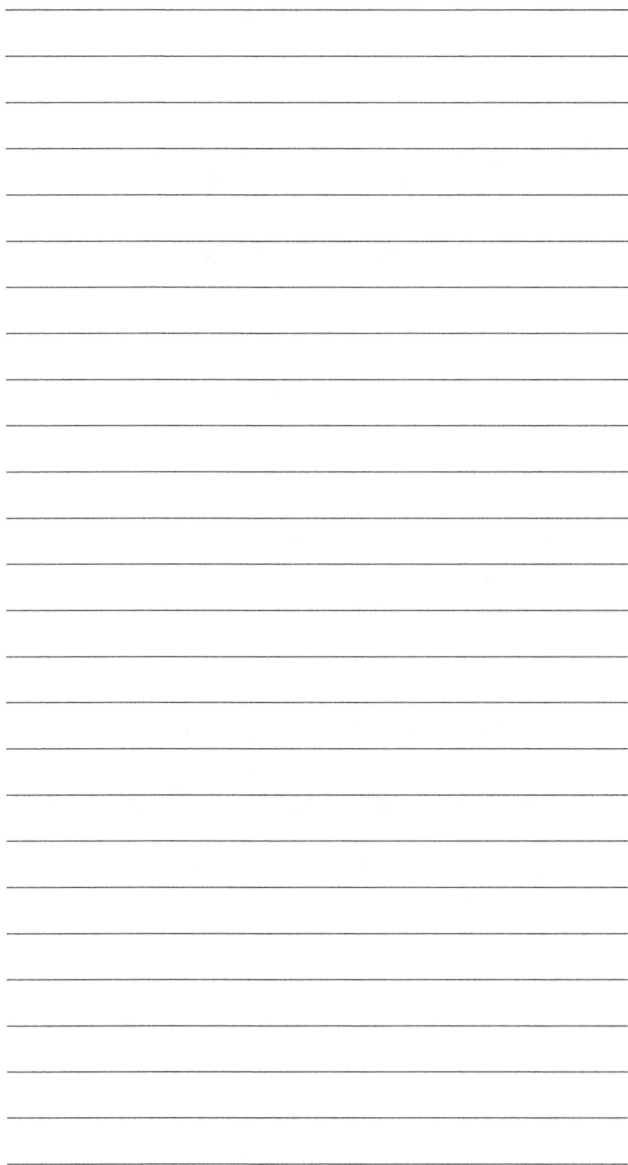

IF ONLY MY MOTHER
HAD TOLD ME...

SOONER OR LATER,
YOU'LL HAVE TO FACE
YOUR WORST NIGHTMARE.
IT'S JUST PART OF THE JOURNEY.

#100

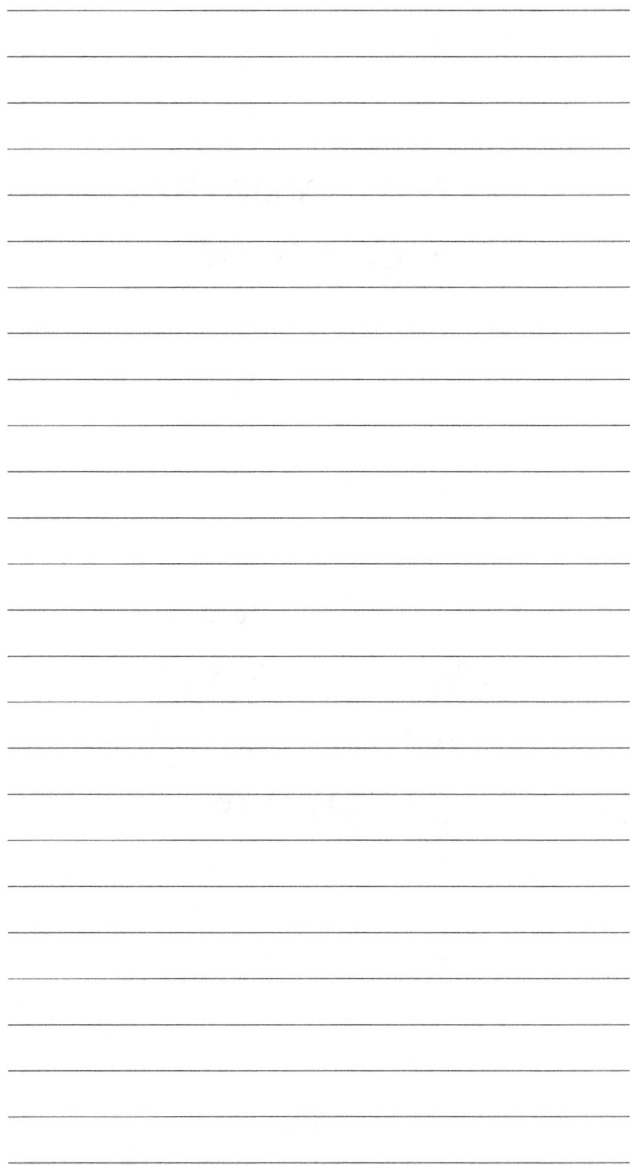

IF ONLY MY MOTHER
HAD TOLD ME...

THE WORLD
DOESN'T NEED FIXING.
YOU CAN GO OUT
& PLAY NOW.

#101

ABOUT THE AUTHOR

Dr. Rosie Kuhn is an international life and business coach, trainer and speaker. She resides on Orcas Island in the San Juans with her sweet dog, Gracie. Contact Rosie via her website for coaching, training and/or speaking engagements.

www.theparadigmshifts.com

Are you interested in more products connected to this book and it's contents? Please go to:

www.ifonlymymotherhadtoldme.com

MORE BOOKS BY DR. ROSIE KUHN

YOU KNOW YOU'RE
TRANSFORMING WHEN...

DILEMMAS OF BEING IN BUSINESS

THE ABCS OF SPIRITUALITY IN BUSINESS

SELF EMPOWERMENT 101

THE UNHOLY PATH OF A
RELUCTANT ADVENTURER

Please visit **www.theparadigmshifts.com**
for more information and to purchase books.

www.ingramcontent.com/pod-product-compliance
Lightning Source LLC
LaVergne TN
LVHW051257080426
835509LV00020B/3011